ENOLA

A TRUE STORY OF CHILDHOOD SEXUAL ABUSE

K.D. WEAVER

ENOLA

DEDICATIONS

To my **Mimi**, I hope you are proud of me. Thank you for choosing me. Thank you for loving me. Thank you for believing in me.

To my Pawpaw, for noticing the red flags and speaking out, despite the adversity that came from it. Thank you for always encouraging me to write.
REST IN HEAVEN PAWPAW

To my father, for teaching me how to live a healthy, balanced life and never turning your back on me, even on my worse days.

To my uncle Scott and his family, you are some of the happiest days of my life. Thank you for never missing a beat in it.

To my best friend Kayley, the words between us are not appropriate for this page. I love you. You are my soul sister.

To my husband and my babies, thank you for seeing me through my beautiful days, even the ones when it rains a little. and supporting me during my most important times. Thank you for holding me accountable for writing this book all the times I wanted to quit. You guys are my reason to breathe.

They said it takes a village to raise a child. My village is more like a small circle, and in that small circle lies a mass amount of love, loyalty and trust. I could not do life without you guys. Thank you, so much.

I would like to dedicate this book also, to my former teacher and now lifelong friend, Mr. Roy Shoulders. My life would not be what it is without the overflow of love and guidance that I once received from you, well beyond my years as your student. I owe you so much more than a small space in this book. You are so much more than just an educator. All my love.

Contents

CHAPTER 1 THE DUNGEON 1

CHAPTER 2 THE CHOCOLATE FOOTBALL 2

CHAPTER 3 A TRIP NOT TO REMEMBER 7

CHAPTER 4 SWEPT UNDER THE RUG 12

CHAPTER 5 WEST VIRGINIA, AGAIN 15

CHAPTER 6 A FAMILY INTERRUPTED 18

CHAPTER 7 ACCIDENTAL SLEEPOVER 21

Chapter 8 DON'T TELL DOUG 29

CHAPTER 9 INCARCERATED WITH A SECRET 34

CHAPTER 10 TWO KIDS PLAYING 38

CHAPTER 11 NO SAFE PLACE 41

CHAPTER 12 EASTER IN THE ICU 49

CHAPTER 13 ZERO 1 SIX EIGHT ZERO 54

CHAPTER 15 GRADUATION 66

CHAPTER 16 HEAVEN CRIED 71

CHAPTER 17 LIZZY 76

CHAPTER 18 DISCLOSE THE DETAILS 81

CHAPTER 19 HISTORY REPEATS ITSELF 83

CHAPTER 20 I AM ENOLA WILSON 86

CHAPTER 21 NOT ALONE 89

CHAPTER 22 UNRESOLVED TRAUMA 92

ABOUT THE AUTHOR 96

KD Weaver

ACKNOWLEDGMENTS

During the midst of exposing my sexual abuse and abuser, I encountered a teacher, that I will never forget. We shared one true passion, writing. I wrote to get through my days, and she encouraged me. She told me when I was doing my best, and when I could do better, in such a way that was never hurtful, but inspiring. Mrs. Duffner, I thought of you a hundred times over while writing this book. You once told me I could become a best-selling author, and I think you were right. Thank you for making me that friend that corrects others' spelling. Thank you for always asking me for more. My confidence in writing began with you.

KD Weaver

CHAPTER 1 THE DUNGEON

The room felt more like an ice-cold dungeon. It was cold in the summer, and cold in the winter. There was a tiny window in the room. A small room darkening valence covered it entirely, all but a small crack where the valence met the window trim. This is where a scant amount of light could be seen from the bed of the dungeon. I always stared at that small bit of light while he was hurting me.

I often wondered what was looming on the outside of that window each time I was blankly staring at it. There were a family of squirrels that lived outside of the window. I had named each of them. Mommy squirrel, Daddy squirrel, Brother squirrel, and Baby Squirrel. Uncle Squirrel often appeared but was quickly ran off. Mommy Squirrel protected her small squirrels, but Daddy Squirrel never knew there was a need to. Now, obviously the squirrel family was nonexistent. I projected a deep dark secret onto an imaginary squirrel family outside of the window.

I was merely a five-year-old child that was not mature enough to concept what was occurring inside of the dungeon, but there I was, trapped there for the first time that I could remember.

My mommy told me to run down and show my grandmother how beautiful I looked. I was two hours shy of marching in a parade with my baton team. Moments earlier I had excitedly skipped down my sidewalk, excited for my grandmother to see me.

"Enola?" a seemingly loud whisper emerged from the stairwell. Immediately upon entering my grandmother's home, there was a banister that lined the stairwell. I could see his eyes through the banister posts peeping up at me. "Enola, can you hear me?" He whispered again, this time a bit louder than the last.

"Hi Uncle Latrine, where is Grandma?" I whispered back at him.

"Grandma is passed out, she is drunk. She drank too much of that bad stuff again. Come down here Enola." He invited me into the basement.

I had been there before, many times. Nothing struck me as odd about it, after all I was five, he was my uncle that loved me. I had no idea my entire innocent life was about to change that day. I had no idea what he was about to steal from me that day. I innocently accepted his invitation to come downstairs.

"Mommy said I have to come back in an hour." I told Uncle Latrine.

1

KD Weaver

I was dressed from head to toe in a purple fleece lined sweatsuit outfit. It was the week before Halloween, and I had long awaited my first parade. I was the smallest girl twirling a baton on the team. I had worked extra hard to be a part of the Halloween parade. My mother had packed up my Halloween costume to wear over my purple outfit, during the march. I was going as the Statue of Liberty. Everyone loved my costume. My mother always had the best ideas for Halloween.

"I will make sure you head back in time, just come and show me how pretty you look." He began to compliment me.

I enjoyed being the center of attention, and Latrine knew it.

"Well come on Enola, why are you just standing there?" He was still whispering and now softer.

I kicked my dirty white tennis shoes off and headed toward the basement. "Why do we have to whisper?" I asked uncle Latrine. "Grandma can't hear us up there."

"Shhhh---- Enola, stop asking so many questions, come here." He picked me up and laid me down on his bed. "Do you want to play a game Enola? It is kind of like house."

"Yes, I love playing games, can I be the mommy?" I was so excited that someone wanted to play with me. Nobody ever played with me other than my father.

"Yes, and I will be the dad." He agreed. "Do you remember what happened last week, Enola?"

"What?" I asked.

"Remember when Papal had to come up because your mom locked your dad out in the cold rain? She did that because he didn't listen to her, Enola." He began to further explain how our game of house would work. "You have to do what I tell you to, and you can't tell your Mommy."

I nodded.

"You can't tell anyone, Enola. You will get in trouble, and so will I."

"Okay, let's play. I won't tell Mommy." I told him.

"Lay down Enola and let me touch you wherever I choose to touch you."

He pushed me backwards onto his bed. "I am going to close my eyes. It's a game mommies and daddies play at night." He stood up over top of me and stared down at me. "Actually, I'm going to kind of sit on you, Enola."

"That hurts!" I cried out.

"Shut up Enola, I told you we will get in trouble if you tell. Grandma might wake up and hear you."

"No, you're really hurting me." I pleaded with him. "I don't want to play anymore Latrine. I want to go home." I had not lowered my voice.

"Shut up Enola."

[Type here]

ENOLA

He covered my mouth and laid on top of me with only his arms holding him up. Latrine was much bigger than me. His weight on my small body, made it hard for me to breathe. He began thrusting back and forth. I could feel something hard rubbing against my private area. He continued. I did not speak a word. I stared out the window and imagined for the first time that I was that Baby Squirrel, and Mommy Squirrel would come to save me soon. I suddenly snapped out of the new and imaginary realm I had escaped to. I had urinated.

"Damn it! Enola! I told you to shut the fuck up and then you did but you pissed on my bed, take your pants off Enola." The laundry room was just opposite of Latrine's bedroom. He pulled my little purple sweatpants off me.

"I'm going to throw these in the dryer, big baby."

He exited but not for long. He quickly returned to the room.

"Let me see it, Enola." He was demanding.

I had no idea what was happening to me. "See what uncle Latrine?" I innocently asked. My legs were together and bent at the knee as I sat up against the wall on his bed. He grabbed my right leg and pulled me down onto the bed.

"Your pie."

I was really confused. This was the word my mother and her family had taught us young girls to use to describe our private area. My mother told me not to show anyone my pie, but I also knew I was supposed to listen to Latrine.

"I don't want to."

"I didn't ask if you wanted to, wife." He replied.

I don't think we are still playing house, are we?

I reluctantly slipped my beauty and the beast underwear off. He pulled my legs apart. I clenched them tightly back together.

"My sister doesn't love you, Enola." He smacked my face rather hard. "That's why you're always here." He grabbed both of my kneecaps and forced my legs apart. He pushed my legs all the way down. Thy were spread as far as they could go, and it was hurting me. He continued to hold me in place.

"Please stop it, I want to go home and go to my parade." I pleaded with uncle Latrine some more. He was seemingly angry, and I had no idea what I had done. "Why are you so mad at me?"

"Shut the fuck up Enola, you aren't very good at playing big kid games." He smacked me again, this time in my mouth. He had let go of one of my legs and had one hands in his pants now. "Are you going to shut up or be a

3

cry baby Enola?"

I did not dare speak a word back to him.

"I'm pulling out my pee bug and I want to put it in your pie. Enola, can I?" This was another term our family normalized for the male private area. I still did not reply. I knew he should not be hurting me like this. He had started to do exactly what he had just described to me.

"Grandma!" I took the opportunity to yell for my grandmother. "Grandma, help."

She never came.

"Shut up Enola." Uncle Latrine continued to assault me.

Is that the feet of a baby squirrel? Stop baby squirrel, my uncle will hurt you too. I see you baby squirrel. Mommy is not coming.

The tears were streaming down my face by this point. He was moving slow. He was frustrated that he could not get all the way inside of me.

"I can't get in you. I have to stop, your mommy might notice, the way you're crying and all." He got up and exited the room.

I could not help but to cry. The harder he pushed, the more pain that I felt. He returned just a few minutes later.

"Here."

He threw my sweats at me. I stood up and put them on.

"Not so fast, Enola, come here."

I turned to him.

"I won't hurt you next time."

He reassured me he did not mean to hurt me but right before he did, he pinched my inner thigh so hard it would later bruise.

"If you tell on me, we will get in trouble. I don't want to get in trouble." Latrine reminded me.

I looked up at him and shook my head to agree with him. I couldn't hardly speak. I was still about to cry from him pinching me so hard. "I won't tell Latrine." I got it out, barely. I ran up the stairs. I could feel the pain in my vagina when I was walking up the stairs. I did not remember experiencing pain there ever before. I sat down in the floor of my grandmother's living room and slipped my shoes back on.

I heard my grandmother's bedroom door crack open. I knew I had to leave before she saw me. I took off quickly out the front door. She opened it behind me seconds later.

"Enola, baby, you look beautiful!" Grandma yelled, "Tie your shoes baby."

"I don't know how to Grandma." I replied but with my back still turned towards her.

"Well come back, I will do it for you baby."

"No, it is ok." I responded.

[Type here]

ENOLA

"Rude." Grandma yelled back.

I had gotten to the street. I was safe again, at last.

How did an hour and forty-five minutes feel like eternity?

I ran full speed from my grandmother's mailbox to my own where I had met my mother. "I was just coming to get you Enola, I told you not to stay so long. Is Grandma coming?"

"No, she just woke up." I snapped back.

"Enola, why the attitude, get into the car." My mother demanded.

I opened the door and climbed in sideways so she could not smack my rear.

"Get me a Pepsi!" She yelled at my father, who was still in the house.

The screen door was blowing, hitting the house over and over. I was counting the times it hit the house. My father finally came out and closed it behind him. He had a smile on his face, as he was approaching the car to load my bag and wagon into the trunk. This was a night I had looked forward to since August the previous year. My baton coach had promised to let me twirl a baton with fire on the ends of it, at her pool party after the parade.

I had to use the restroom, but I knew my mother would yell if we had to stop. I held it the entire hour drive to the meeting location for the parade. It was a street corner, where there were no commercial buildings present. "I have to pee Mommy." I finally told her. She always told me that I could hold it, as if my need to use the restroom was inconveniencing her whole life. "Mommy, I have to go so bad it hurts.".

"Enola, we are at a fucking parade. Where do you want me to take you to piss? In the alley?" Her demeanor was rude, per usual. "Come on." She grabbed my arm and dragged me behind her. She was walking toward the huge old brick Victorian home in front of us.

"Sorry Mommy." I was sorry. I did not mean to upset my mother.

"Where are we going?" I asked her.

"Unless you want to piss in this yard, I seen an old lady on this porch, and I'm going to ask if we can use her restroom. I don't know why you didn't go before we left, Enola." My mother headed up the old brick steps. She knocked. The sweetest elderly woman answered the door.

"My daughter has an emergency, and she can hardly hold it, could she please use your bathroom?"

She let us in and led us to the restroom.

My mother stood outside of the door while I entered the restroom. I pulled my sweatpants down and climbed up on the toilet. I sat there and after a few minutes, I realized nothing was coming out. I did not actually

5

have to pee. I still felt like I needed to go though. I pushed, and still nothing. "I'm done." I told my mother through the door.

"Damn it, Enola, you didn't even go. I could hear you." My mother was furious. "You begged me to bring you to a restroom, and you didn't even go. What is wrong with you Enola?"

She berated me about it for the next hour until it was time for me to march. I marched for an hour that night. I do not recall one single detail of the parade. I went to the party afterwards. I don't remember being there. I do not know whether I got to twirl a baton with fire on it or not. I know there was a pool, but I know I did not swim in it. I was slightly bleeding, and I did not want anyone to know. The only memory I have is trick or treating. It was held prior to the parade start. I was with Bubba. I held his hand and smiled. Life as I knew it, would never be the same again.

[Type here]

CHAPTER 2 THE CHOCOLATE FOOTBALL

"Enola! Are you laughing at me?" My mother was in my face, accusing me of mocking her while I had slept. "What is so funny Enola?" She kept asking the same question, over again.

"Nothing Mommy, I was sleeping." I finally realized I had just been awakened from a deep sleep by my severely intoxicated mother. I knew so much more than the other kids my age, despite my daddy, his family and their attempts to keep me innocent. I could tell by the look my mother had in her eyes, she was drunk. I had already learned when to know she was beyond the point of caring what my answer was. I was going to be wrong regardless. "I'm sorry Mommy." I bit the bullet early and accepted fault.

"Didn't I tell you that you aren't allowed to sleep in here, Enola?" My mother was screaming at me. She turned to exit her bedroom, at which point I followed her. "You aren't a fucking baby, Enola." I followed her into the kitchen. I knew at this young of an age, going in my bedroom and shutting the door would only upset her further. I sat down across from her at the kitchen table. I remained quiet. I knew the less I said, the better off I would be.

I was looking past my mother at the empty box behind her on the counter. My Mimi had bought me a chocolate football during one of our infamous shopping trips we took earlier in the week together. I was staring at that empty chocolate box so hard. I wanted to move it so bad, I focused until I was dizzy. I had attempted to get my mind to move it for me. Nevertheless, it did not move. There it was, the empty box, just waiting on my mother's discovery. She turned to get a Pepsi out of the fridge. She noticed the box. I panicked. She stomped away from the kitchen.

"Did you really let her eat that chocolate football?" My mother smacked my father across the face to wake him up. I heard the loud smack. "Can you fucking hear me?" She slammed the bedroom door.

He reluctantly looked up, only to see her coming towards me. I put my head down on the table attempting to avoid her obvious anger and fit of rage.

"Enola are you stupid? Why would you eat this whole football?" She acted as if I had eaten the forbidden fruit. She was furious. "Enola, why did you eat this?"

7

I was no amateur at holding my feelings in. I had carried a deep dark secret for two days leading up to this night. I had a heart of steel and feelings that would remain buried, and very much alive, for many years to come. I remained completely silent. I knew she was about to throw an intense and possibly violent fit about this football situation. My stomach was in knots. My mother was dressed in white from head to toe, she was wearing a matching sweatsuit outfit. I stood up to hug my mother, hoping that she would accept my apology. "I'm sorry, Mommy."

My mother didn't have a chance to answer me.

"Shut up Cassidy!" My father had entered the conversation, abruptly.

My father rarely stood up to my mother. I know now he feared her as much as I did. There had been countless evenings that my mother had stayed away from home until late at night, or even not returned home at all. Either way, she disturbed all the peace when she finally decided to come back. My father always tried to hide it from everyone. They knew. Everyone knew. My brother and I certainly knew.

My father believed she had been getting better in the years prior, as my brother was born. He was only a year old, sound asleep in the other room. My father was already upset she had left that evening. "Why do you even bother, if you don't want my children, leave them alone, and leave me alone too." My father exploded on her. "Who were you out with tonight anyways?"

"You won't do this to me right now. I am not feeling well." My mother knew he was right and for some reason, she did not want to fight right then. It was a rare occasion she would walk away from a confrontational situation, especially one that she had initiated.

By this point I was standing at my mother's side, I yawned, and leaned in to hug her. She squeezed me tightly, as if she were putting feelings into the hug. I never really felt love in my mother's touch. I knew it from a young age. She did not love me as other moms did their children. She loved me, how my grandmother loved her.

"Good night, Mommy," I headed towards my bedroom. I didn't dare attempt to lay back down on the floor beside my brothers' bed, which was on the same side of the bed my father slept on. I was peacefully asleep there before she came home and disrupted it. Where I would have never bothered her.

"Enola!" My mother screamed so loud again.

I jumped as she startled me, but I had not even turned around before I felt her smack me across my bottom. My vaginal area would now always be sore as a small child. Her swat to my rear, hurt, and I couldn't dare tell her.

"Mommy-" I tried to plead with her to calm down, but I was quickly interrupted.

[Type here]

ENOLA

"I told you not to eat this fucking football, Enola." She screamed as she grabbed my arm and smacked my bottom again. "It is all over my sweatshirt from your mouth."

"I'm sorry Mommy." I couldn't have held my tears back, but I wanted to. I know now I was nearing the point of an anxiety attack, displaying severe symptoms. "Please stop Mommy." I saw her slightly raise her arm backwards.

"Just look at my brand-new white sweatshirt! Do you see it?" She was in a drunken fit of rage.

My other grandmother, Mimi, my father's mother, spoiled my mother. Everything my mother had, she described as 'brand new'. She came from poverty, so she valued the things that were given to her, and Mimi had just bought her the sweat suit outfit, when she bought mine for baton.

"Cassidy, you can get another sweatshirt. Enola honey, go to bed." My father stepped in between my mother and me. This was something he had become a professional at, within a few short years of my existence. I headed quietly into my room. I did not want to upset my mother any further. My father picked up the mess my mother had made during her episode, and then came to tuck me in. Every night he brought me a glass of water and tucked me in. On the seldom good nights, my mother would then enter the room and tickle my neck and sweetly whisper, "snuggle buggle baby." Tonight, she didn't. In fact, she didn't even tell me that she loved me. My father had already put me in bed once. I woke up in my bed afraid. It was something I had newly started experiencing after Latrine had started sexually abusing me.

I simply went and laid in the floor for security. This is what set my mother off originally. The sight of me, in her floor, as if I were not worthy to sleep in the floor.

The next morning my mother woke up and did not remember anything from the night before. I suppose my father had gotten up early and washed the chocolate out of her sweatshirt so I wouldn't get hit over it again.

"Why is the baby crying?" My mother angrily asked.

"Maybe because he wants to feel the comfort and love of his mother, Cass. You were here and now you aren't." My father withheld nothing that morning.

"You sound just like your mother. It's ok for a mother to go out and have a good time, you know?" My mother defended herself.

"You don't go out for good times. You go out to find men and get so shit faced that you don't remember beating your own child." My father always reminded her when she went too far with me. It was one of the

9

reasons why she envied me so much. She could not stand the love my father had for me. It angered her when he defended me.

"I have only been out twice since I had Bubba." She offered further defense for the things she had been doing. My father knew it was the beginning to something that would likely never end. Him and I had lived this hell with her once before. I was three weeks old when she left my father and I to attend spring break in Florida. She didn't really pick up on the whole 'mom' thing. She didn't know how.

"He is only a year old, Cass, you talk about your mother, but you are becoming her!" My father just fueled the fire into an explosion with that remark. He proceeded towards my brother's bedroom.

"My mother is an alcoholic, that is a disease that she cannot control, how fucking dare you, and in front of Enola?" My mother always responded in such a way that made her somehow, appear to be the victim. My mother's eyes were still blood shot from the excessive drinking she had done the night before. "Enola, you love Grandma, don't you?" She made eye contact with me.

"Yes Mommy, Grandma is my best friend." I replied. I loved both of my grandmother's. Grandma was young, and full of drama. Mimi was an older modest woman that always had it together. She was much classier than Grandma. "You love her more than Mimi?" My mother tormented me with questions like this.

"No, I love Mimi the most." I answered her with fear, but honesty. I never lied about the love I had for Mimi. Mimi is a kind soul, the type of woman that makes you feel at peace while you are with her, even when you had to return to hell. "Mimi is my angel." I continued.

Pawpaw always called Mimi an angel, she was the center of his whole world. My parents came from completely opposite families. Southern class and southern trash. I wasn't sure why my mother was asking me these questions. Things had suddenly gotten quieter.

There was a knock at the door.

"Let me guess, your mommy is here to check on me?"

My mother opened the door. She had seen Mimi's old boat of a car pull in our driveway from the living room window.

"Knock, Knock!" Mimi always announced her presence when arriving to our home this way. A double knock followed by the actual words. I was always so excited to see Mimi. "Do you want to go shopping, Enola?"

"Yes! I do Mimi."

Mimi and I regularly went shopping together. Pawpaw worked hard and Mimi and I spent his earnings without a second thought.

"Come on baby." Mimi patted me on the top of the head and proceeded into the kitchen. "What has happened in here?" Mimi demanded an answer

[Type here]

from my father. He always defended my mother. I knew he was going to lie. I also knew I was going to be told to back that lie up.

"It's a mess because we are a family with two children, mother." My dad was annoyed she was adding to the already awful morning. Mimi knew it too. I told Mimi everything anyway. The day prior I didn't miss a detail when telling her all the things they had been fighting about. I had even provided her with a letter my mother wrote to my father. Mimi was the main character in that letter. It was long and descriptive, almost like a story. My mother envied Mimi. As a small girl, I didn't realize it wasn't Mimi, it was that Mimi wasn't her mother. My grandmother was awful, and my mother was robbed of that healthy relationship she deserved. Everyone deserves a Mimi.

"Bullshit." After a few seconds went by, Mimi returned the answer my dad was hoping would remain a thought in her head. "You always lie for her. I'm taking Enola, and I'll be back. Clean this mess up. It isn't good for the kids." Mimi picked me up onto her hip and we headed out the door. I opened Mimi's car door and climbed in. I finally felt like I had reached pure safety. I did not have to walk on eggshells around my Mimi and Pawpaw. They were safe, good people. Mimi got into the car. "Do you think I oughta' go back in and get Bubba, Enola?"

"Yes." I answered without hesitation. Mimi got back out of the car.

"Buckle up, I'll be right back." Mimi said.

I buckled my seat belt and adjusted my underwear. Now each time I sat down after a visit at my grandmother's, I felt pain in my vaginal area. I thought about telling Mimi what had been happened to me. I began to prep myself to tell her. My uncle told me I would be in trouble, but Mimi didn't discipline me. I took a deep breath. I dropped my cabbage patch doll onto the floor of the car. I removed my seat belt and bent over to retrieve it. "What are you doing, Enola?" Mimi opened the car door.

She startled me, and I quickly sat up and hit my head on the glove box. "I dropped my Georgie, Mimi." I replied. Georgie was the name of my doll. "I got her though." I buckled Georgie in the seat belt beside me. Mimi loaded Bubba's car seat into the car. I looked back at him. I remembered Latrine said he would suffocate him if I ever told. I wanted to cry, but I didn't. I was fierce, and I was strong. I swallowed the secret again and I wouldn't even be considering bringing it back up again for many years to come.

CHAPTER 3 A TRIP NOT TO REMEMBER

It had only been a year or so since our last trip to West Virginia. I was seven years old. I felt like a big girl. I packed my own bags and was ready to get there. Despite the things that uncle Latrine did to me the last time we were there, I had warm fuzzy feeling when I was in my great grandmother's home. I love Christmas lights and she let hers hang along the stairs to her attic all year round. My great grandmother Margaret was a deep-rooted hillbilly. She was a kind woman, the kind you seldomly come across. Not even my grandmother spoke ill of Grandma Margaret. She lived in the same home she had raised my grandfather and his eleven siblings in. It was a small two bedroom. My aunt Faye lived with her as an adult. She cooked from sunup to sundown. A person never went hungry at Grandma Margaret's. I loved Faye. I only had the opportunity to meet her a few times as a young girl, but every time I seen her, I knew I would feel loved. Aunt Faye hugged me and told me how beautiful I was. On more than one occasion she had also told me if something were happening that shouldn't be, I could tell her. *I wish I had. Oh, I wish I had.*

Upon arrival, our family gathered in Grandma Margaret's small yard, fenced in by a rusty old chain link. I sat at the picnic table that was inside of her garage with several of my cousins in attempt to avoid my uncle Latrine once we got there. He noticed me right away.

"Hey Enola. Guess what I saw today?" Latrine approached me kindly.

"What Uncle Latrine?" I asked.

"There's a super cool comic bookstore down the street. I saw a barbie comic book… The dolls even pop out." Latrine persuaded me.

"No way. There are dolls in it?" I was excited.

"Yeah. Tomorrow I will buy it for you." Latrine said, "if you are good."

"I will be Latrine." I scooted closer to my cousin Skyla on the bench. She was a few years younger than me. After a minute or so went by I could feel myself sticking to her, it was hot outside, it felt like it was one hundred degrees.

"Why do you get everything Enola?" Skyla asked.

"I didn't get nothing." I replied.

"Uncle Latrine likes you better than the rest of us."

"Whatever, stop it." I got up from the picnic table. My father was standing with Papal talking a few feet away. I walked over to him and leaned on his leg. There was a group of kids playing football in the street, there was a fire going, there were a few gathering in the garage, but I wanted my dad where I felt safe.

ENOLA

"What's your thing chicken wing?" My father looked down at me.

"I'm bored, Daddy." I responded.

I felt a tap on the shoulder. I turned around. It was Latrine.

"Want that comic book now?" He asked.

I looked up at my father.

Sure, I wanted the comic book, but what was the catch? I knew Latrine was not doing this just to be nice. Latrine was never nice to me.

"In a little bit." I replied softly.

"Come play, Enola. What's wrong?" Latrine asked.

"Go play baby." Papal pushed me towards Latrine.

Papal did not know, and neither did my father at that point, that he had just pushed me right into the arms of danger. I was not safe with Latrine. In fact, our recent encounters had become extremely dangerous. I did not want to go, but I was afraid to cause a scene.

"Come on stupid." Latrine grabbed me and pulled me through the garage once he got me away.

"Everyone is outside Latrine; I want to play outside." My cousins had scattered from the table we had filled up moments prior. I pulled my arm back away from Latrine once we reached the door entering the home.

"Did you just bully me, Enola?" Latrine grabbed my arm back and pulled me through the doorway.

"No, I don't want to go inside Latrine." Latrine had a tight grip on my little arm. It felt like an Indian burn he was clenching me so tight. He pulled me towards him. He grabbed my hand and placed it on the outside of his pants, directly on top of his semi-erect penis.

"Come on, Enola." He grinded his teeth together and dragged me to the living room. "Sit here, Enola. Don't you dare move." Latrine shoved me onto the couch. He got up and pulled each curtain back to look outside. There were nine windows in the home. He looked out each one, and then around the house. The house was unoccupied, despite the amount of family members that were present. "It's just us in here." Latrine was clearly relieved.

"Can we play outside?" I begged.

"No, we can play upstairs, like last time." Latrine smirked.

"I don't want to Latrine."

Latrine leaned towards me. He pushed my legs apart and pinched the inside of my thigh. It was still bruised from the days prior. He pinched my little thigh, every time he sexually assaulted me. This last two weeks, it had been daily. Sometimes, multiple times a day.

"Ok, Ok." I quickly gave up on my negotiations.

13

"Come on stupid." Latrine pulled me up the stairs.

Latrine made me lay down on the floor. He again opened the curtain and checked outside. He pulled it closed again. He walked back over to me and began to undress himself. He had an old black t-shirt on, and baggy jeans. He was holding his penis in his hand, thrusting his hand back and forth.

"Take your pants off, Enola."

"No, I'm scared." I objected.

"Take you pants off, Enola. I'm not asking you." He demanded.

I laid completely still. Latrine leaned down and pulled my jean shorts off me. They had lady bugs patches on them. Mimi had ironed them on, right before we had left. Latrine forced my legs apart and began to assault me once more. I looked out the window. The curtain was blowing with the wind. I could hear the laughter from my family outside. I could hear my mother's voice over the others. She was giggling and having a good time. I knew my father was right beside her. Neither one of them had any clue what I was enduring, feet away. Nobody did. I wondered if Bubba was asleep. I don't know how much time went by, but just before Latrine got up off my small body, I seen a squirrel run across the phone wire.

Baby Squirrel always seemed to appear

"Ouch. Latrine, ouch." I let out an abruptly loud cry. My tears were flowing, and the pain was unbearable. My already bruised thigh that he had already pinched again that morning, felt like it was on fire. Latrine had never pinched me as hard as he just did.

"Shut up, Enola." Latrine placed his hand over my mouth.

"I want my mommy." I was letting it out, even if he didn't want me to.

"Too bad. Let me dress you, Enola."

I laid there completely still. I was still wearing my panties that had the days of the week printed on them. It was Thursday.

"T-H-U-R-S-D-A-Y," Latrine spelled out the word.

"I can dress myself." I tried to grab my panties from him.

"No, I will dress you, like the cry baby that you are, Enola." He placed my underwear back on me, and then my jean shorts. He had never removed my light up tennis shoes. I saw them light up red as I lifted my leg for Latrine to put my shorts on me. I didn't even know I still had them on. "Don't tell. Let's go get your comic book, Enola."

Latrine got dressed and wiped the sweat off himself. He grabbed my hand gently and led me down the stairs. He instantly searched the room.

"Still just us?" I asked.

"Just us, Enola. It will forever be, us." Latrine responded. Latrine still held my hand. What looked so innocent to my family, was far from innocent. I was hurting and nobody knew it. Latrine walked through the groups of people until he found my mother.

14

ENOLA

"Enola what happened to that hair? Come here." My mother said.

I walked over to my mother, but I never said a word. I had a head full of wild curls and it was not all that uncommon for my mother to need to fix my ponytail. If she only knew what really happened. She pulled my hair tightly back into a large bun on the top of my head.

"Thank you, Mommy." I spo

"Can we go to the comic bookstore Cass?" Latrine asked my mother.

"Sure, keep a hold of her." My mother was so trusting of Latrine.

"Here's some money. Get her whatever she wants, she is bored." My father handed Latrine a twenty-dollar bill.

"Ok." Latrine accepted the cash and stuck it in his pocket.

We walked down an old brick road to the comic bookstore down the street. It was in town. Grandma Margaret lived just outside of Huntington. The area felt old, but welcoming. We approached the comic bookstore, and I could see the Barbie book in the window. I was so excited.

"I want that!" I pointed at the comic book.

"I know. I am going to get you that." Latrine said.

We entered the comic bookstore. There were no workers in sight. Latrine headed to the comic book I wanted right away. He removed it from the window and stuck it up his t-shirt, quickly before anyone greeted us. He then began to look around.

"Hey, you guys new in town?" A man emerged from the back room.

"Nope, our grandma lives here." Latrine answered.

"You lookin' for anything specific?" He asked.

"Just the barbie book." I blurted out.

Latrine nudged me.

"Oh, there's a new edition in the window. It has pop -up dolls and everything." He said.

"We have to go." Latrine grabbed me and pulled me toward the door.

"Did you steal?" I whispered.

"Shut up, Enola."

We walked at a faster than normal pace down the street. There was an alley between two old buildings. He grabbed me and pulled me into the alley, where he found a space behind a dumpster that could not be seen from the street.

"I'm scared Latrine."

"Shut up and come here." He pulled me behind the dumpster.

Latrine pulled the comic book out of his shirt and sat it on the ground beside us. He sat down on his knees and began to caress my legs with his fingertips.

15

"Be quiet and I will give you this."

I did not say a word. I was standing straight up against a brick wall. Latrine started to kiss my legs. He pulled my underwear to the side along with my shorts and began to lick my vagina. I was embarrassed. I could feel myself turning red, I felt hot. For a moment I thought I would vomit, but I held it in. I was looking all around to see if anyone could see the two of us. I did not see a soul. Latrine continued for a few minutes. I didn't make a sound. This was a new game, that we had never played before.

"You don't like that?" He stopped and stood up.

"No." I replied.

"Here is your book." He handed me the comic.

"Thank you."

Latrine grabbed the barbie comic book back out of my hands. He opened it to show me the page where the pop-up dolls were. I was excited despite the second sexual assault in an hour occurring moments before. He ripped the page out. My heart sunk. He ripped every single doll out of the book and ripped it up.

"Enjoy your stupid book." He handed it back to me.

CHAPTER 4 SWEPT UNDER THE RUG

"STOP!" I screamed at the top of my lungs, "JUST STOP!"

It was too late. He did it anyways. Latrine had balled his fist and swung at me just as I had screamed those words. I covered my little face with both arms to shield myself from another blow. My grandmother was gone, and my grandfather was on the road working. It was just Latrine, Bubba, and me. Bubba was upstairs asleep in a pop-up play pen. I crawled toward the door. Uncle Latrine grabbed my legs and pulled me back into the room. This was not a rare occurrence. In fact, it had become regular. I often had carpet burn on different parts of my body, my mother scolded me not to let anyone drag me when we were playing. She never dreamt then that it could have actually been done on purpose, or did she?

"You want to sit there and make fun of me? Curt was my favorite artist." Latrine reprimanded me further.

I had backed myself into the wall his bed sat against. I was curled up with my knees to my chest, scared. He took a few steps towards me and hit me again. This time he hit me in the side of the head. I fell over, off the bed. I somehow managed to escape the room and ran upstairs and locked myself into the restroom. The lock on the outside was able to be picked with a penny, turned, and whoever wanted in, was in. I knew I was not safe there. Latrine quickly got the door open and grabbed me. I was so small he was able to pick me up and pin me against the wall holding my shoulders.

"Let me down, please." I cried. Uncle Latrine had just reached adulthood. He was much bigger than me. He never responded to me, he put me over his shoulder and took me back downstairs. Bubba had begun to cry. I knew he could get out of the playpen, and I was terrified he would fall down the stairs. Nevertheless, Latrine ignored my brother's cries and began once again to sexually assault me. He ripped my underwear taking them off.

"These used to say F-R-I-D-A-Y." He spelled out the word.

My mind had shifted its focus from Latrine to the emptiness outside the window. There were no squirrel feet or shadows present to ease my mind. I could feel every ounce of pain he inflicted on me that day. From the punches to the face, him kicking me in the stomach, to sexually assaulting me. I felt everything that fateful Friday. Every last thing.

"You like it, Enola." Latrine asserted while he continued to sexually assault me.

17

"You are hurting me."

"Cry baby Enola."

"Latrine." I let out a squeal.

I knew the sound that had just submerged from my body was one he had never heard before, because I had not heard it either. He really hurt me this time.

"Blood." I began to hyperventilate.

"It's fine Enola. That is something that happens when a man becomes man."

"I'm going to be in trouble." I was panicking. Clearly.

"You can hide it. Wear black pants. It isn't much." Latrine became agitated.

"I'm scared." I was scared and hurting. Severely. Latrine went upstairs where my grandmother had a drawer of clothing, that was all mine and got me a pair of black sweatpants.

"You are here for two more days. It will stop before you go home."

I put the black pants on. I could not seem to calm myself down. When I cried hard, my entire face would cover in red spots. On top of that, I was struggling to maintain a steady breathing pattern. I was experiencing a full-on anxiety attack, years before I realized what it was. Latrine was mad at me, more mad than usual. I thought he was going to kill me. He picked me up and slammed me into the wall once more.

"You have to stop this." He demanded.

I heard what sounded like a loud fumble outside of the bedroom door. My first thought was Bubba. Latrine dropped me to the floor and opened the door. I gasped. It was my grandmother. She had fallen down the stairs. She was sloppy drunk. She smelled like something sweet, but I knew it was alcohol. The 'bad stuff' that always excused her behavior. Latrine shut the light off in the bedroom, hoping Grandma wouldn't notice. The television was on, so there was plenty of light through the room.

"By God damn what were you doing to her?" My grandmother said as Latrine picked her up from the floor.

My grandma and I made eye contact. She looked directly into my broken little soul, and she knew it. She knew I was hurting. A large tear fell from my already wet eyes. I wanted so badly to tell my grandmother the details of what had just happened to me, but all I could think about was Latrine hurting Bubba.

Bubba was my entire world, from the time he was born, until we parted much later in life. Bubba brought light to my mother. She loved Bubba in a way she did not love me, at least that is how she displayed it. I wanted to be just like my mother. What she loved, naturally, I loved. How she dressed, I dressed. She was always rather agitated with me, but I still had a strong desire to be around her. I loved my mother more than anything. Her pride and joys were also mine, Bubba. I never wanted anything to happen to him. At this time, that meant continuing to carry the weight of the deepest secret. The only thing I knew for sure now, was Grandma was carrying it too.

My mind had gone completely blank when my grandmother stumbled into my cries for help. I disassociated myself into the other realm that I so often visited. All I could see was the family of squirrels, happily running away together down the wires. Suddenly I snapped back into reality. My grandmother was carrying me up the stairs. She kept asking me over and over what happened, I didn't ever answer her. She already knew or she wouldn't have been asking.

I did not verbally disclose the details of my sexual abuse to my grandmother. She saw the red flags and she ignored them. She put a movie on in her spare bedroom and told me to get a good night sleep, and then she never mentioned the episode after.

The next morning grandma asked me if I wanted to take a bath. I always took a long, hot bath at Grandma's. Latrine quickly told grandma that I should take a shower, because he needed one too, and he would like some hot water. He knew the chances of my grandmother opening her shower curtain to look at me were slim, but she may come in and sit if I were taking a bath. She agreed and a shower it was. After my shower, I balled my bloody underwear up and put them in the bottom of my overnight bag. When I got home, I put them in the back of my closet. My mother discovered them years later and assumed I had hidden my first period out of embarrassment. She never knew they were actually evidence to a heinous crime.

CHAPTER 5 WEST VIRGINIA, AGAIN

I couldn't have been beyond nine or ten years old. I remember the smell like it was yesterday, I wanted to puke. My aunt Faye was frying chicken livers and onions on the stove top. My mother had warned me about the old West Virginia hillbilly cookin' that her family would still be doing. My father and I were picky eaters, and my mother knew it. We went grocery shopping immediately when we arrived in town. Latrine and I had pizza rolls in the oven. Latrine and I had claimed out space on the stairs that the attic of my great grandma's tiny home. We were the first ones in the living room, we were not waiting on chicken livers. My grandmother brought us both our pizza rolls and a Pepsi.

"Don't fall Enola," she said.

There was not a handrail on the side of the stairs that face the living room, only on the wall lining them. The other side was open.

"Ok grandma." I smiled at her.

"Want to go up there?" Latrine pointed toward the door at the top of the stairs.

"What's up there?" I asked.

"A futon for guests and storage. Don't you remember, Enola?"

"I'm scared." I knew what would happen if I went in there with Latrine.

"Don't be, come on." Latrine grabbed me.

I willingly stood up and followed him.

"Grab your pizza rolls, Enola."

"Ok Latrine, I will." I giggled.

"Shut the door, Enola." Latrine said as I came back into the room with my pizza rolls.

I turned around and the shut door.

"Lock it." Latrine demanded.

"Why?" I asked.

"Lock the door, Enola. You might know why if you think about it really hard, stupid."

I walked away from the door without locking it.

"I guess I will." Latrine got up and locked the door.

I wasted no time to start eating. I quickly stuffed two pizza rolls in my mouth. I was starving. I had begged my parents to stop and get me nuggets on the way to West Virginia. We did not stop. Latrine grabbed my plate of pizza rolls and opened the window. He dumped the pizza rolls which landed on the roof. "Enola look." Latrine waved me over to him. I curiously walked over to Latrine. "Come on, we can get on the roof, did you forget?"

"I'm scared Latrine." I was scared and my memory had repressed my earlier visits to Grandma Margaret's. I couldn't remember much of anything.

"Don't be, come on." Latrine and I scooted out onto the roof. It was flat where we were sitting. I could see my family below us, but they could not see us. It was dark outside. They were having drinks. We were there for a large family reunion.

"Enola... shhh!"

"Sorry." I had just loudly sneezed.

Latrine looked at me. I knew the look he was giving me. He saw an opportunity and he was going to take it, and he did not care about my feelings. I would lay there, once more, helplessly and take whatever he was going to do to me. I would not yell; I would not cry. I knew the routine now. Sure enough Latrine pushed me back into the window.

He laid me down on the futon and began to assault me. There was a glass Christmas tree lit, with the most beautiful old lights. I stared into the lights unto they became haze. Latrine assaulted me a little longer than normal. He got up twice to check and make sure my parents and grandparents were still outside. The third time he got off me, he grabbed his sock off the floor and placed it around his penis. "Enola I wasn't supposed to do that in front of you. I always go to the bathroom and finish at home." Latrine stood there holding the sock over himself.

I didn't speak a word. The pain I felt each, and every time Latrine assaulted me was real. It felt like a knife stabbing in and out of me for hours after the assault. I often bled lightly. I used my fingers to check. I was not bleeding. I slipped my night gown back on. The sleeve was inside out, and I struggled with it.

"Need some help kid?" Latrine laughed.

It wasn't funny. I didn't answer him.

"Too cool for me like everyone else?"

I remained silent. I finally got my arm through the sleeve. The night gown had red cherries all over it. It had been my grandmother's and then my mother's and now it was mine. Latrine ruined the sentiment behind the night gown that night. I searched for my panties.

"You need these? F-R-I-D-A-Y." Latrine spelled out the day of the week printed on my panties.

"Yes." I was humiliated.

"Too bad, go without them, and don't tell either, Enola."

21

He stuffed them into his pocket and left the room. He had signaled for me to exit with him, however, I refused. I grabbed a blanket and laid down on the futon he had just raped me on.

"Enola, you can't sleep up here. You have to sleep with your mommy."

My aunt Faye had appeared. "You alright kiddo?"

"Yeah why?" I became defensive.

"You look like you're going to be sick, Enola, you sure? Let's go find your mama."

"Don't tell her I look sick Aunt Faye."

"Enola, what's wrong? Who was up here with you sweetheart?"

"Latrine."

"Did he hurt you, Enola?"

I started at Aunt Faye. I thought briefly about my answer. At that moment, I heard Bubba let out a cry. He was having a tantrum. "No, he didn't." I had suddenly remembered Uncle Latrine's threats to take my brother's life if I ever told on him for assaulting me. I was afraid of Latrine. He hurt me. I did not want him to hurt Bubba.

CHAPTER 6 A FAMILY INTERRUPTED

I held my brother tightly behind my closed bedroom door. He cried onto my chest. Out of all the things that I had experienced in my eleven years of life, feeling my brother's pain was the absolute worst of it. He was young, precious, and pure.

I was young precious and pure at one time too. I would do anything to keep Bubba that way. Just the night before I had attended a movie with my mother and her boyfriend. I think I knew about my father's demise well before he knew.

"It's okay Bubby." I whispered and kissed his forehead. He was sitting sideways on my lap, and I had both arms wrapped around him. "I love you and no matter what happens with Mommy and Daddy, we will always be together." I squeezed him a little tighter as we listened to what seemed like an active war zone outside of the bedroom door. We had heard the bombs dropping many nights leading up to this.

"You guys—" My father attempted to barge into the bedroom. My back was against the door. "Let me in." He calmly pleaded. I moved my brother onto the floor beside me and scooted away from the door far enough for my father to enter the room. He shut the door behind him. "Daddy is moving out." My father with no preparation, dropped that bomb on my brother. Once again, I already knew this was coming. In fact, I had prayed for this day. I knew I could seek safety with my father if I could just get him to safety first. I had told my father in the days leading up to this bombshell, I had overheard my mother telling her my aunt Bozo on the phone that she was telling my father he needed to move out. I had listened to the lies my mother used to back her own selfish wishes up. She wanted my father to leave because she had a boyfriend, but she was not going to tell anyone the truth. I had to listen to her lie on my father, on several occasions, when I knew the truth. As I did this day, I knew he was leaving, before he knew. My brother understood every word my father had just spoken, and he was so upset, he could hardly breathe. "Come here Bubby." My father reached for my brother and pulled him close. "Come here Enola." He pulled me near him as well. "Everything is going to be ok, we all still have each other."

"Are you fucking kidding me? I tell you that you're moving out and you tell them five minutes later, before you even know if you're moving?"

My mother entered the room screaming at my father.

How dare her. Here she was trying to make herself the victim again. "Not going to say anything?" She continued to badger my father. He still didn't offer her a response. My mother walked out of the bedroom. My father quickly got up when we heard the front door loudly slam.

"She's gone again." My father sighed. I had crept into the hallway behind him without his knowledge. I had heard my father speak those words many times. I hurried back to the room so that he didn't know I heard him. My father rarely showed any negative emotion. He didn't cry, but he cried that day, heavily.

"It's ok Dad. I want to come to your house, so make sure there's a bedroom for me." I sat down on the couch beside my father. "I love you Dad."

"I love you too, Enola." My father began to heavily cry.

The night went by rather quickly. My mother didn't return until late.

My father had cooked my brother and I meatloaf. He boxed up a piece and told me to take it to Papal. It was my father's way of communicating with my grandfather, without telling on my mother himself. He knew I wouldn't miss a detail when I told him her business. My grandfather wouldn't ask leading questions, but If I gave him information, he opened a thorough investigation. He knew my mother was a mean alcoholic. He also knew she was unfaithful to my father on many accounts. He had been married to my grandmother for thirty-some years, and he knew my mother was an exact replica of her, and he tried well into my mother's adult life to correct her misbehavior.

"Be right back." I grabbed the plate covered with aluminum. My dad always sent food down to Papal this way. "You think he will like this Dad?" I chuckled. Papal complained about everyone's cooking.

"No, he will probably talk shit." My father laughed.

I shut the door behind me and headed to my grandparents' home. I got past the bushes that lined my neighbor's property and saw that Latrine's truck was not there, which meant I could visit with Papal without worry. I let out a huge sigh of relief. I needed Papal. I walked up onto the porch where Papal met me at the door.

"Hi Tadders." Papal was excited to see me.

"Hi Papal, Dad made you some meatloaf." I handed him the plate. He lifted the aluminum foil and sniffed the meat loaf. "Papal, it's good." I laughed.

"There ain't no shit way in hell this is going to taste like anything but ass. Your daddy can't cook." Papal decided the meatloaf was nasty before he ever even tasted it. "Go get me a fork and a bottle of ketchup, if you haven't borrowed it." We always borrowed their condiments, never to return them.

"Ok." I chuckled again. I headed into the kitchen and opened the fridge. "Yep, you have enough left for this meatloaf." I handed Papal the ketchup.

"Not enough ketchup in the world to flavor some things Tadders. You and Bubba eat ketchup on everything because neither your mommy or ya Daddy can cook for shit." Papal responded.

Holy shit. He is right. Bubby and I eat ketchup on absolutely everything.

"Is it good?" I asked Papal after his first bite.

"Not too bad but tell him I said it's awful." Papal smacked his knee and chuckled.

"Papal, guess what?"

"What Tadders?" Papal interrupted me. "I ain't no guesser, what ya got good Tadders?"

The comfortable feeling left the room. Papal knew by the look on my face I was about to give him unpleasant information.

"Dad's moving out." I quickly got it out.

"What in the hell did you say?" Papal sat his fork down on his plate.

"Dad's moving out. He just told us. Mom got mad and left." I responded.

Papal didn't finish the conversation I had started. He picked up the cordless phone that he always had sitting beside him while he was home. I knew he was calling my mother. Papal put his coat on and stepped outside. It was snowing rather hard and freezing cold. I could not hear what he was saying through the door.

"What in the damned hell is the matter with her Enola?" He came back in.

Enola? Did Papal just call me Enola? Not Tadders? Papal is sad, I can see it, Papal is so sad.

"I don't know Papal." I quietly responded.

"She oughta bring her damned drunk ass home and be a mother to you children. She will regret this bullshit with your Daddy." Papal spoke without thinking. "I'm sorry Tadders, you don't need to hear any of this. Get your shoes, I'll walk you home. I want to check on ya Daddy." Papal pointed at his boots. I grabbed them and handed them to him.

"Where's grandma?" I asked.

"Same damned place your mama is, probably." He responded.

Papal and I were headed back to my house. "Papal, can I tell you something?" I asked.

25

"No." Papal joked

"I hope I get to stay with Daddy." I confessed.

"Your mommy means well Tadders. She doesn't know how to be happy. We gotta get her there one day. She needs you and Bubba." Papal guilted me, and I see it now. He knew my father was a better fit to care for us. He had to know. I was shocked by this answer.

"Mommy is mean Papal."

"Tadders," Papal was agitated and interrupted me, "I ain't gonna dog   your   mama   with   you,   she   is   only   human   too."

CHAPTER 7 ACCIDENTAL SLEEPOVER

I slammed my bedroom door, knowing now it was an attempt to infuriate my mother to the point she would call off work. I would rather her throw a fit and blame me for missing work than have to go to my grandmother's. It did not work. My mother opened the door, she put me across her knees and spanked my clothed bottom. She didn't know when to stop and often I think she hurt me more than she intended to. This specific incident was one of those times.

"You will do as I tell you! You are ten years old." My mother screamed at me. She was nearly out of breath, "End of discussion, Enola." I could smell the sweet liquor she had drank the night before. It was still fresh on her breath. Her eyes were blood shot as if she hadn't slept in days. She always looked fed up and frazzled.

"Can I just go to Mimi's please?" I pleaded with my mother, even after the spanking I had just received. My brother sat in the floor outside of my door. He was loudly crying from all the commotion going on. Luckily for me he was crying. My mother redirected her attention toward him. She picked him up and quickly declined my plea to go to my safe place.

"Walk your god damn ass down that street to your grandmother's house, Enola." I walked down the hallway, down the stairs, and up the sidewalk gracefully that day. I knew what was going to happen to me now and I knew the wrong attitude would make it worse. I reached my grandmother's driveway and seen my Papal. I skipped towards him. The fear left my body when I saw Papal. I knew Uncle Latrine would not hurt me while Papal was there.

"Papal!" I yelled as I now ran toward my grandfather. He was on the porch swing smoking a cigarette and drinking a Pepsi. "I missed you Papal!" I sat down on the swing beside Papal.

"Hi Tadders." I am still unsure of the reason behind it, but that was my chosen nickname from Papal and my mother's whole family addressed me as such. He gave me a great big hug. "Whatcha been doing?" Papal asked.

"Hi, Enola." Latrine opened the door.

I ignored Latrine, and answered Papal, "Just twirling my baton, playing with bubby and playing house with uncle Latrine." Uncle Latrine stared at me, I felt a bad feeling radiating from his eyes, as if he wanted to gouge mine right out.

"Let's go up and see Bubby, Tadders." Papal said.

He grabbed the red rider wagon he used to pull me around the neighborhood in when I was a much smaller girl. "Hop in baby girl." I hopped into the wagon without question. I couldn't believe he was going to pull me in it. Latrine motioned for me to "zip it." I nodded. He did not have to speak to me to scare me.

"So, nothing is new Tadders?" Papal asked as he pulled me up the street.

"Nope nothing."

My mother had just put her bags into the car and was getting ready to bring my brother down. Papal beat her to him.

"Bubba." My grandpa picked my brother up raised him above his head. "You sure do got a big head Bubba, just like your mama." Papal chuckled.

"I have to go Dad." My mother hugged my grandfather and passed my brothers stuff off to him. Papal sat it in the wagon. "I'll see you later Enola." My mom slammed the car door and off she went. My mother was always late for everything and always in a rush. She didn't ever tell me that she loved me. I always wished that she would.

"Well guess it's just us for a few hours." Papal said.

"Will Mommy be back in a few hours Papal?" I asked.

"No Tadders, I have to take a load out West. I will be gone for a few weeks." Papal answered me. I could tell by the tone in his voice he hated to be on the road again so soon. Papal loved all of us grandkids, and he spent an equal amount of time with us, even though it made Grandma mad.

"I don't want you to go Papal. Can you wait until mommy gets back?" I begged Papal not to leave in just a few hours.

"I have too honey; Grandma will be home by the time I leave." He said. Papal was still pulling me in the wagon. We had made it back to his driveway. He made a loud beeping noise and backed the wagon in beside the house, with me and Bubba still in it. I giggled. "Come on Tadders." I followed Papal back to the porch. "Whatcha think?" Papal asked Bubba. Bubba missed Papal too. He climbed up on his lap.

"Boo ba doo boo boo." I ran my tiny finger down my brother's nose. He smiled. "I love you little Bubba." I said as I leaned into give him kisses on the forehead. Bubba was one of the best things that had ever happened to me. He made mom happier, and she knew how to love Bubba, at least it appeared that way compared to how she loved me.

Bubba made his way over to me. He was sitting on my lap. I moved my leg and almost dropped him. He was only half as big as I was. ". Your mommy would beat you if you accidentally hurt Bubba, she actually likes him." My grandfather chuckled at his rude comments. He was an old hillbilly from West Virginia. Some said he lacked common sense, but for some reason, even from a young age, I understood his dark sense of humor.

"I will Papal." I assured Papal; I would never let anything happen to Bubba. If he only knew how far I had gone to protect Bubba.

ENOLA

Latrine opened the screen door again. It startled Bubba and he began to cry. "It's ok baby brother." The screen door was cast iron, the latch made a loud noise when it released from the house. "I love you so much Bubba." I pulled Bubba close to me when I saw Latrine. Latrine had numerous times threatened to end Bubba's life if I had ever spoke on the abuse I was enduring at his hands. He told me if I even thought about it, he would kill him. I had thought about telling on him so many times, I always wondered if he knew.

"Come here Bubba." Latrine said. I had a hold of Bubba for dear life, and I didn't let go of him to Latrine. "Are you fucking dumb Enola, I want to play with him." Latrine snapped at me.

There wasn't a chance I was going to hand Bubba to Latrine. Ever. I knew Latrine was a bad man, and I would not let him touch Bubba.

"Who the hell do you think you are?" Papal got up and confronted Latrine, who was standing over top of me with his arms out, as if he were going to be handed a baby. Papal didn't give Latrine time to answer the question he had just asked him. He smacked him across the face. "Take your fat ass to the basement." Papal demanded Latrine. Latrine was eighteen years old at the time. "Did you hear me dumb ass?" Papal raised his arm again.

"I heard you." Latrine started crying and walked into the house. "It's not fucking fair. Enola gets babied and I'm always the bad guy." He spoke loudly to my grandfather as he walked down the stairs.

"Damn it boy, shut up." Papal said. Latrine did shut up too. He was afraid of Papal, and I had seen firsthand the reason why. Papal's mood changed after he smacked Latrine and sent him inside. I was still holding my brother, who had started to cry from the yelling.

"It's ok baby." I said.

"Come on over here Bubba. Tadders you can play." Papal took my brother out of my lap and sat back down on the porch swing. I skipped up the street to get my sidewalk chalk out of my mailbox. I had placed it there a few days before when it started to rain. I drew on the sidewalk for hours. Papal sat on the porch and held my brother. Uncle Latrine never came out of the basement after his and Papal's confrontation.

"There's your grandmother, Tadders." Papal said, "Get out of the driveway dummy, you know Grandma she might be drinking, she might hit ya ass." I grabbed my chalk and quickly sat down in the yard so Grandma could pull in. Grandma parked and shuffled things around, clearly leaning to the passenger side of her car.

"God damn it, told you Enola, she's drinking. Look at her hiding her bottle." Papal headed towards the car with my brother on his hip. "I see the brown paper bag Jean." My grandfather called her out.

"Oh, you do not you big sucker." My grandmother responded. My grandfather always defended her lewd behavior and said she only spoke in such a manner when she was drinking, but she was always drinking. "Get out of my face Latrine." My grandmother yelled. She did not want him to smell the alcohol on her, so she made loud comments implying to the neighbors he was doing much more than he was. "Don't touch me sucker." She said.

"Jean, you know I wouldn't touch your drunk ass, the way you would lie to the law if the Karlisle's called them, I'd be in prison for the rest of my damned life." My grandfather started to defend himself. "How the hell are you going to watch these babies when I leave Jean?" He sighed, "Ya old piece of dirt. Dirt has more value in my damned life than you do right now."

"Are you kidding me Latrine? Jr. can help me out, but I only had a few drinks."

She always lied about her level of alcohol consumption. She had my mother shared the use of this common lie. We knew how much they had drank by the way she was acting, not a tough system to figure out. She had more than a few drinks and Papal knew it.

"Go in there and take your ass a nap, Jean," Papal said. "Sober up a little before I have to leave these babies with you." Grandma didn't say anything back to him. She headed to the bedroom and passed out. It wasn't the type of nap Papal was referring to, it was a drunken black out.

"I'm sleepy too Papal." I sat down beside him.

"Go take a nap." Papal said.

"Will you get my blanket Papal?" I asked him. He had brought in a comforter that was originally kept in his semi, because it was my favorite blanket. It was kept folded up, in the top of their bedroom closet, just for me.

"Sure, will baby." Papal said. He headed into the bedroom or the blanket. He tossed it and a pillow onto the couch when he returned. "Sweet dreams, Enola."

"If I am sleeping Papal, wake me up so I can give you a hug before you leave." I said as I laid my head down on the pillow.

"I will honey." Papal reached his pinky out, and pinky promised me. It was something the two of us did when we were making a promise.

An hour turned into four, and I woke up to no sign of Papal, and no sign of Bubba. I sat up and rubbed my eyes as I yawned. I could see grandma in the kitchen. "Where is Bubba grandma?" I asked.

"Mommy came and you were sleeping, I told her you could just stay here tonight."

Grandma, why, why did you offer for me to stay here I want to go home.

ENOLA

I knew grandma's feelings would be hurt if I asked to go home. She took everything personal, and she wouldn't understand why I didn't want to stay, and she wouldn't be afraid to bully me for weeks had I asked to go home.

"OK." I replied. "Can I have some ice cream with syrup on top?" I asked Grandma. Papal and I always had ice cream covered in syrup when he was home from his long trips in his semi. I had slept much longer than a short nap and missed ice cream with Papal before he hit the road again.

"Sure you can Enola." Grandma sat her cigarette in the glass ash tray and walked into the kitchen, where she lit another cigarette while she made me ice cream. It was usual for her to have a cigarette burning in each room, some burned to the butts, and she never even remembered having them lit. Grandma got my ice cream, two scoops of strawberry with extra chocolate syrup. "Here you go, grab a tray and you can eat it downstairs with Latrine, he's watching a movie."

"I'll stay up here grandma." I sat my bowl down on kitchen table.

"Oh ok, well don't make a damn mess, Enola." Grandma said. She opened the fridge and poured herself another drink. She had just awakened hours earlier from her spurt of day drinking, and here she was, at it again. I knew from a young age when Grandma drank alcohol, she became what was equivalent to be the devil. "What are you looking at me like that for, Enola?"

"I'm not grandma." I answered her and giggled in an attempt to lighten the situation that had suddenly became dark. My refusal to hang out with Latrine downstairs enraged my grandmother. Latrine was a boy of very few friends. He was incredibly quiet, withdrawn if you will. He was the chubby poor kid on the block, and he was often bullied over the way he looked and dressed. Of course, my grandparents weren't poor, my grandma was a functioning alcoholic that worked long days in the hot summer sun. My grandfather was only home every few weeks, he was an over the road trucker. "Can I go back to bed now, Grandma?" I asked her, I had quickly finished my ice cream.

"How could you possibly be tired? You will wake up and be up all night long if you go to bed now." Grandma began reasoning with me to stay up for a few more hours. "I'm stepping out for a few hours, Enola, you and Latrine will be fine, and I don't need you telling your know-it-all Mommy my business either, clear?"

No Grandma, please don't leave. Do anything… but leave.

I pleaded with her in my mind, although I never actually spoke a word. "Ok." I answered. I was afraid of my grandmother just as I was my mother. She had a very mean tone, and a permanent 'disgusted with you' look on her face. "Where are you going Grandma?"

"To shit, hopefully the cows will eat me, Enola." She always answered me that way. I still don't know where she went, but I know the hogs didn't eat her.

"Don't be gone long, Grandma." I innocently demanded.

"Oh, hush it, you won't miss me too long." She poured herself another drink. I could see the blank looking starting to present itself through Grandma, it was the same look my mother had when the evil was about to exit her mouth and move within her actions.

I sat down on the couch and watched Grandma put her shoes on. I kept looking at the stairwell hoping to God Latrine wasn't going to appear, and sure enough he did. There he was. His eyes were beaming into my soul from behind and in between two wooden bars on the banister. He stood there silently preying on me, without saying a word, right in front of my grandmother. Just as he did the first time he had taken my innocence, years before.

"What in the shit are you doing?" She finally noticed Latrine and he scared her. "I will be back, you need to watch Enola for a little bit, be nice to her. And I don't want your sister in my business, so I don't need you guys to tell her that I left. Handle it, Latrine." Grandma stood up, grabbed her black leather coat, and exited the home, locking the front door behind her. She knew the danger was behind the locked door, and the outside was my safety and my freedom while visiting her. I don't know why she bothered locking the door.

"Come play, Enola." The door had just latched when Latrine demanded that I join him downstairs.

"I thought you were watching a movie, Latrine." I questioned his motive.

"I am, it's part of playing house, you know, Enola, it's a movie I think you will want to watch this one." He responded.

"No, I am going to lay down up here." I did just that, laid down on the couch and covered myself up in my special blanket. Papal told me when I had the blanket, it was like a hug from him and that I should feel loved and safe. I covered my face and thought of my grandfather. I heard Latrine coming up the stairs. I froze.

"Get the fuck up and play house with me Enola, you little bitch." Latrine was standing over top of me. The tone of his voice terrified me. The older I got, the worse he spoke to me.

"No." I wasn't going into that dungeon willingly this time.

Latrine grabbed my leg and pinched my inner thigh near my vagina once more. He had usually done this after he assaulted me. "Stop it Latrine." I demanded.

"No, you don't make the rules, I do, Enola." Latrine pinched me, in the exact same spot, over again. "Don't fight with me, Enola."

I didn't fight back either. Latrine pulled my pajama bottoms off. Suddenly he was on top of me again, only this time, we were on the couch right in my grandmother's living room. I could see the branches of the trees moving in the front yard. I could see the headlights of the cars passing by. I could hear the show my grandmother had left on the television playing. I could hear and see everything but Latrine. I had blocked him out and escaped to my other realm again, almost as if I were hallucinating.

"If you tell, I will kill Bubba, and it won't take long. I will lead him into the woods and tell him there's a dinosaur from J-Park, and I will leave him dead, like those dinosaurs." Latrine always threatened me after he assaulted me. "Do you understand me, Enola? You let me play with you like this, you will be in trouble, and Bubba will die. Don't you dare tell on me, Enola."

I laid there silently and didn't respond. I knew Bubba had recently grown to love J-Park. This bothered me, so much. I sat up and covered myself back up with my special blanket, so I wasn't exposed anymore. I was waiting for Latrine to go to the basement so that I could get dressed. He got to the top of the staircase and before he headed downstairs, he came back and grabbed my pants and took them with him. Swinging them on his finger above his head in a cowboy style motion. I laid down anyways.

What am I going to tell Grandma if she comes home, and my panties and pants are both off? I am going to be in so much trouble. What do I do?

My exhausted body couldn't function often after he assaulted me. I would tell my mother I was ill for days sometimes. I had fallen asleep and a few short hours later, I woke up to Latrine inserting his finger inside of me. "Stop it, Latrine. We already played house. I am tired." I pleaded again.

"Do you like it rough, Enola? If you listened, I would be gentle, and you would love it." Latrine was asking questions that I didn't know how to answer. I was merely a little girl still. I blankly stared at him, which seemed to quickly upset him. "Are you dumb, Enola?"

"No, I'm tired and I want my one of my parents. I want to go home." I demanded.

"Your mommy doesn't want you or your Daddy, that's why she is never home and doesn't care where you are, Enola." Latrine had leaned over and picked me up. "You are sleeping in my room whether you like it or not, Enola.

"Ok, I will walk." I was too afraid to fight back. Grandma's quick "errand" had lasted all night.

Latrine dropped me to the ground. He kicked me in the side, "Walk down the stairs, retard." He said.

"Don't hurt me uncle Latrine, I will be a good girl, please don't hurt me again." I grabbed the railing alongside the staircase and walked down to the dungeon, and willingly. I didn't want Latrine to hit me or kick me. Once we reached the dungeon Latrine picked me up and threw me on the bed. I turned on my side as if I were going to go to sleep. He jerked me onto my back. "Please stop." I begged him.

He didn't sympathize one ounce with me, "I just want to lay on top of you and dry hump you, Enola."

I knew exactly what he meant, he had "dry humped me" many times prior. "I can't breathe when you do that to me Latrine." I didn't want him to lay on me. I really had to use the restroom. "Can I go pee?"

"No, Enola." Latrine climbed on top of me. He began thrusting. I closed stared into the crack of the window, there was no light from the outside. I wondered where baby squirrel was and if mommy and daddy squirrel were protecting her.

"What in the actual hell are you doing to her, Latrine?" My grandmother had busted through Latrine's locked bedroom door.

"Playing." Latrine responded. He had thrown the blanket over top of me, and I felt him remove his finger from inside me. I didn't even know he had put it there; I was focused on the whereabouts of the squirrel family outside of the window.

"I don't want to see you playing with Enola like that ever again, Latrine." Grandma said. She closed the door and exited the room.

"Close call." Latrine said.

I felt big tears streaming down my face. "Can I go upstairs now that grandma is home?" I asked.

"Why are you crying Enola, we didn't get in trouble, and you liked it." Latrine always attempted to convince me that I liked the things he was doing to me.

"I won't tell, but I want to go upstairs." I replied.

"You can sleep in here, she shut the door, you're fine." Latrine wasn't going to let me leave that bedroom.

"Ok." I rolled over and watched the analog alarm clock on the dressers' hands move slowly, all night long.

CHAPTER 8 DON'T TELL DOUG

The panic had set in. I was in the closet of my grandmother's spare bedroom. My clothes were downstairs. I had escaped the dungeon and locked myself in the bathroom before my uncle unlocked the door from the outside with a penny. I don't know why I always ran to that bathroom for safety. He easily gained entry, each time. He demanded that I come back to his bedroom. I refused. A loud knock at the door had interrupted my uncle from beating the life out of me, half naked, for running from him. He panicked and told me to move into the spare bedroom. Once we got into the spare bedroom, he violently shoved me into the closet. My head hit the back of it.

"If you come out of this closet, I will kill you." He made me a pinky promise, just to mock Papal's reoccurring pinky promises to me. I don't know why in the terror I was, I offered him my pinky.

"Please get my panties and pants Latrine." I begged.

"Shut the fuck up and get in the closet, Enola." He shut the closet door.

I heard a familiar voice. It was Doug, Latrine's best friend. They headed toward the basement. I couldn't leave the closet. I didn't have anything on from the waist down. My sweatpants were in Latrine's room, with my Saturday panties. I had a pair with each day of the week printed on them, well into my teen years. An hour had gone by. I finally heard Latrine coming up the stairs.

"Latrine." I whispered quietly. "Latrine, please get my clothes."

"Enola, is that you?"

Oh shit. It is Doug.

I remained quiet.

"Enola?" Doug whispered again.

"Yes, please don't tell Latrine you saw me."

"Enola, I won't. Do you have pants on?"

"No, Doug, please don't look." I pulled the closet door back shut. It was a foldable door with no lock on it. Doug went into the restroom without saying another word to me, and back downstairs, as if he never encountered me. So I had thought. I heard someone coming back up the stairs, loudly. I could tell it was an angry stomp. I knew it was Latrine's stomp.

"Enola, I fucking told you to be quiet. I was going to make him leave." Latrine yelled at me before he even opened the closet. I was expecting him to have my clothes in his hand, he did not. "Come on Enola." He grabbed my arm.

I fought him. I swung at him. "No, Latrine, I don't want Doug to see me naked. I don't fucking want you to see me naked either, Latrine." I felt like I had reached my breaking point. This situation with Doug, had become too much.

"Yeah right Enola, why do you keep coming to Grandma's then?"

"Because I'm always grounded, Latrine." I yelled. I was still kicking at him as he was pulling me out of the closet by my leg. I could feel the carpet burning my back again.

"Well, we're playing house and you are grounded here too." Latrine said.

"I'm eleven years old Latrine, I don't want to play your sick game of house anymore." I cried. I don't even know if he understood what I was saying.

"Come on sweet girl." He picked me up.

"Please stop." I didn't have the strength to fight Latrine anymore. I knew that he was going to do whatever he wanted with me, regardless. He carried me into the dungeon and laid me on his bed.

"Look at the TV, Enola." Latrine demanded.

I grabbed the blanket and pulled it over me. I glanced up at the TV to see a woman nearly my mother's age with two men, all completely naked. I looked away.

"Do you like this movie, Enola?" Latrine asked me. He pulled the blanket back off me.

"No. Doug, help me." I looked at Doug. He had one hand in his pants and shook his head at me. He shook his head no. I could not believe it. I could have never prepared for what was going to happen to me next.

"Doug isn't helping you, Enola. Spread your legs." Latrine forced my legs open. "Such a cute little thing, you should shave it though." Latrine said. "Go ahead Doug, you can touch her."

I was mortified. I had known Doug since I was born. I had just started growing hair on my vaginal area, and I had anticipated the embarrassment of Latrine pointing it out, but nothing could have prepared me for him doing it in front of Doug.

"No. You know what I want to do." Doug backed up towards the closet. I was crying.

"You never touched a girl before have you Doug?" Latrine asked.

"Doug don't do this." I cried.

Latrine smacked me, "Shut the fuck up, Enola." He grabbed Doug's hand and forced Doug to touch my vagina. Doug enjoyed what Latrine had just given him access to: my innocent young body.

ENOLA

"Lock that door." Latrine moved Doug out of the way. He almost acted as if he were jealous.

"Stop it Latrine." I screamed.

Doug locked the door.

"Now you did it, we are in trouble, Enola." Latrine forced himself on top of me.

I looked over at Doug. He was reaching for something in Latrine's closet. He finally pulled it out. It was a video camera, wrapped up in sweatpants. Doug turned it on and began to film Latrine assaulting me.

I stared at the crack on the window. I felt the tears streaming down my face. I wondered where baby squirrel was. I wondered if Mommy squirrel had taken her and ran away with her. Suddenly my mind went blank. I had passed out while I was still conscious. I don't have any other way to describe it. The realm I had normally escaped too, couldn't remove this kind of pain from my body. I was suddenly awakened.

"Enola, did you hear me?" Latrine shook me really hard. "Enola!"

I didn't respond. I could hear Latrine, but I couldn't respond.

"I'm out of here, I never seen anything, I never did anything." Doug announced his departure. He took the video camera with him and exited the basement using the door that led to a stairwell outside of the house. He was gone, and quick.

Just as Doug exited and Latrine reminded him not to tell, I lost consciousness. My mind refused to process what had just happened.

"Enola." He smacked me. "Enola, wake the fuck up are you ok Enola?"

"Latrine?" I felt my heavy eyelids trying to open. I had processed everything that had just happened, I just was not fully coherent. I'm not sure what type of protection mode my body entered, but it did.

"Enola, what happened?" Latrine seemed worried. He picked my leg up and started to dress me. I felt him lift my back up and pull my panties back up over me. He also put my pants back on me. They had my name embroidered in them with my soccer number. He ran his fingers over the threads. "I'm sorry, Enola."

I felt lifeless. I guess my little body couldn't handle anymore abuse at the hands of Latrine. I physically shut down. Latrine had violated my small body over one hundred times over the last six years.

"Enola, are you bleeding or anything?" Latrine asked. He stuck his hand down my pants to check for himself.

"Oh my God, what are you doing to her?" My grandmother had arrived home, without Latrine realizing she was there. She had opened the door without knocking, again.

"Playing." He quickly responded. This was the third time my

grandmother stood over my hurting body and asked Latrine what he had done to me.

"Enola, are you playing?" Grandma asked me.

My grandmother never took me to the side and asked me these questions in private. She always put me on the spot in front of Latrine. She had physically caught him with his hands down my pants and asked me if I was playing.

"Yes, she's playing Mom, are you serious right now?" Latrine answered my grandmother on my behalf.

I shook my head.

"Latrine, come upstairs, we need to talk." My grandmother left the room and headed upstairs. The stairs were directly outside of Latrine's bedroom door. I watched her shadow until it disappeared.

"Don't fucking tell on me, Enola." Latrine leaned down and whispered angrily in my ear.

"I think Doug already did." I whispered back.

I hope Doug told on you. Please have let Doug told on you!

Latrine was still leaned down beside me. "Don't tell, Enola." He pinched me hard on the inside of my thigh once more. At least it was through my clothing this time. It still hurt. Latrine anxiously ran up the stairs to talk to Grandma.

I laid there, still, hoping this was the end of what had become normal to me. I prayed again. I could hear my grandmother scolding Latrine. I sat up on Latrine's bed and gathered myself. I felt sick, severely sick. I got up and couldn't bare walking up the stairs, the thought of doing so itself overwhelmed me. I sat down on the couch. There were music videos playing on the television.

"Stay out of Latrine's room, Enola!" Grandma was only a few inches from my face bent down yelling at me. I do not even know when she shifted her anger towards me. I didn't have the energy to argue back with her.

"Ok grandma." I replied.

"Just like your Mommy. You always want to be in a place you shouldn't be. And then… then when someone hurts you, you cry wolf and blame them." Grandma continued. "Why would you be doing that with your uncle, are you sick, Enola?"

Oh my god. Help me, God. She does know. I don't want Latrine to have sex with me why would she even say that? She knows. I knew she knew.

I turned over onto my side, facing away from my grandmother and the television. I had tried to convince myself she didn't know; despite the number of times she had caught him. Grandma was still scolding me. She was blaming for the years of sexual abuse I had endured at her sons' hands. I suddenly realized; I really wasn't the only one who had carried a dark

ENOLA

family secret. Grandma was carrying it too, with pride. I had been in denial about this, for far too long. I don't know what she was saying by that point, because I had tuned her out. I had exited my body and went outside with the squirrel family. Into my other realm.

Baby squirrel was so much bigger now, and mommy squirrel was not anywhere around. Mommy squirrel, where could you be?

I was worn out. My developing body was tired. I had endured so much in eleven short years of life. I had fallen fast asleep on the couch. I was suddenly awakened by the sound of Papal's steel toe boots stomping, angrily, down the stairs.

"Latrine, get your sick ass up." Papal was screaming at Latrine.

I didn't know uncle Latrine was sick, I hope I don't catch it.

"Get you god-damned sick ass up, Latrine." Papal repeated himself. I could see what was going on. The couch was in line with Latrine's bedroom door, I could see directly in his room. Papal had a hold of Latrine, and now he was beating the life out of him. I could see the fear in Latrine's face. It was much like the fear I had so many times seen on my own in the mirror.

"Enola, get Grandma." Latrine pleaded for my help. He was holding a deck of cards in his hands still. He had managed to escape Papal, he headed up the stairs. Papal grabbed ahold of Latrine's foot and pulled him back down the stairs. He hit him so hard the deck of cards went flying all over the living room, and Latrine was bleeding from his nose and mouth.

"Grandma is sick too." Papal had stopped beating on Latrine after the last blow, but he was still terribly angry. "You're both fucking sick. Come on Enola." I was scared. I didn't understand why Papal was so upset. I laid there and pretended to be asleep still. Papal had been so focused on Latrine, he hadn't actually paid attention to the horrific state I was in. "Enola honey, get up." Papal picked me and carried me up the stairs, where we were quickly met by Grandma.

"You going after ya Papal next, Enola? I know you wear those little uniform skirts to turn the men in my house on." Grandma was again inches from my faces, even when I was in Papal's arms. "You think you are hot shit, just like your Mommy." I could smell the alcohol on Grandma's breath, and strong.

"Jean, sit down and shut the god damned hell up." Papal jerked me away from Grandma. He walked me over to the couch. There was an upstairs living room, and one down. Grandma kept the upstairs completely spotless, and we kids were made to stay in the basement. It angered Grandma that he had sat me on that couch.

"Latrine is your son, named after you. He is your flesh, and he is your blood. Cassidy isn't." My grandma reminded my grandfather right in front of me, that he had no biological ties to me. He had raised my mother since she was a baby. This angered my grandfather further.

"Jean, Tadder's is my grandbaby. She was my first grandbaby, and her mama was my first daughter, how dare you?" She had intentionally redirected Papal's attention. "If Latrine hurt this baby and you knew..." He did not finish his sentence. In fact, he never finished the sentence.

"I wouldn't let Latrine hurt Enola. They're two kids, playing." Grandma responded.

CHAPTER 9 INCARCERATED WITH A SECRET

I could smell Mimi's French toast all the way from my bedroom. Bubba and I had different kinds of days when they started and ended with Mimi. French toast was the only breakfast Bubba and I mutually liked.

"Are you up, or are you up?" Mimi asked as I slowly entered the kitchen. "You turned into a sloth or what, Enola?" Mimi giggled. Mimi never insulted us. Every word she spoke to Bubba and I was sincere.

"I'm a sloth." I cracked up laughing and pulled my blanket all the way over my head. Bubba laughed. "Slothy, slothy, slothy!!" I tickled him. "I love you little dude."

"Do you want your syrup hot or cold?" Mimi asked me. This was a controversial subject within my dad's side of the family, do you refrigerate syrup, or warm it up?

"Hot." I answered her, "Bubbas too."

Mimi served us our French Toast. Bubba had bananas cut up on his plate. I was a picky eater, he ate anything. I didn't like fruit.

"Want a bite, Sissy?" Bubba held a piece of his banana inches from my face and laughed some more.

"Yeah sure." I grabbed the banana. "Airplane. Wheeeeew... Crash!" I put the banana in Bubba's mouth. Bubba would outgrow my silliness and love soon, and I knew it. I enjoyed every moment with Bubba.

"Cops." Bubba said.

"You are going to call the cops because I put your naner back in your mouth?" He always called them naners.

"No cops at grandmas Sissy." Bubba was facing the front window. Mimi and I both had our backs turned towards it.

"Oh my goodness, lots of cops." Mimi said.

I got up and stared out the window. I saw the cops lining my grandmother's driveway, and the house across the street was being taped off with yellow caution tape. I wondered what was happening. Mimi was at my house because my mom and grandparents were in Las Vegas for the weekend. My dad was working, and Latrine was home alone.

"I wonder if Latrine is home." Mimi said.

"There he is." I responded. Latrine was being guided down the driveway in handcuffs. There was an officer on each side of Latrine. I felt a

41

whirlwind of emotions.

"That little donkey probably got in trouble without Jean in town watching wiping his ass." Mimi didn't cuss often but I knew she had just called Latrine an ass and thew an insult. Mimi hated Latrine, and so did Pawpaw. Years early Pawpaw had voiced a suspicion that he was concerned with Latrine's behavior towards me. I think Mimi believed him, but my mother quickly shot it down.

"I hope not." I responded. I loved Latrine so much, despite everything he had done to me in the years leading up to this moment. I knew Latrine was beat regularly by my grandfather. He had no patience with him. I also knew my grandmother drank and verbally abused Latrine, to the point I believe he felt like he was nothing. A part of my sympathized for him, even when I realized he was wrong. Latrine glanced up at my living room window. I locked eyes with him. The look of fear filled his face, the same look I had seen after Papal beat him so many times. I started to breathe heavily.

"Are you alright, Enola?" Mimi noticed my upset.

"Is Sissy ok Mimi?" Bubba asked curiously.

"Honey?" Mimi placed her arm on my shoulder.

"Yeah, I'm alright." I didn't know what Latrine had done, but I knew what he had done to me. I knew it was wrong. I wanted him to stop, but I didn't want him to get in trouble. I didn't want to get in trouble with him. "I'm alright I promise." I followed up. Mimi was worried, I could see it. She was staring at me, as if the secrets I had been keeping were laying on my shoulders for the public to see. "What?" I asked.

"Enola, you look like a ghost. Forget Latrine, you have no involvement with whatever he has done, have you?" Mimi asked.

I can't answer that until I know what he has been arrested for, after all that video tape Doug has would land Latrine in a cop car.

I'm looking away from you now Mimi, stop hounding me. I wish I had no secrets to tell. I wonder where baby squirrel is now.

"No." I said.

"I didn't think so, but you look like somebody just placed the weight of the world on your shoulders, Enola." Mimi was worried. "Is there something you need to tell someone?" She asked.

"No Mimi, I promise." I hated lying to Mimi, but I just did.

Mimi had called my aunt Bozo. She lived five minutes from us, in a rundown trailer park. I saw her pull up. She noticed Latrine in the cop car right away. She knelt beside the car. The window rolled down where she was able to have a conversation with Latrine.

"Should I go snoop?" Mimi asked. She was going to go snoop either way, so I'm not sure why she asked me. "I'm going. I'll be back, watch Bubba." Mimi quickly put her shoes and coat on and headed down the street. I never took my eyes off her. She had gotten a quick update on Latrine and was back in the living room before I knew it.

"What did Latrine do?" I inquired.

"Apparently he and a few others were robbing the man across the street and got caught." Mimi responded.

"Mr. Ladkins?" My worry turned into anger. "Are you serious?" I asked.

Latrine had bullied Mr. Ladkin's son so far, that he had attempted suicide months prior. His name was Alex. He had been walking his dog down the street a few months before and the dog escaped the leash and pulled me from my bike. It bit my side when I tried to ride away from him. My father was present when the incident occurred, but Latrine still bullied him over it. He was the only person permitted to hurt my in his eyes, I guess.

Alex's dog was put down after it bit me. Alex loved his dalmatian. He had long wanted that dog. I always felt guilt over the situation, even though I was the one bitten. It was not Alex's fault; he surely did not bite me.

"Yeah him, but the robbery isn't the worse part." Mimi wasn't leaving any details behind, "Mr. Ladkin's was home and suffered a heart attack, they scared him so bad."

"Where is Alex?" I asked.

"I didn't see him, Enola." Mimi replied.

I picked the phone up. I knew Alex's number by heart. He was secretly broken, just like me. We had shared each other's problems under the night sky the last summer. The summer of 99'. I was ten years old. I learned so much about Alex, and I loved him, dearly. I called twice with no answer. I was worried. I didn't want Alex to be left alone. I was afraid he would hurt himself. I sat the phone back on the hook and continued to stare out the window at the situation unfolding. All our neighbors were outside.

The cop car that Latrine was in slowly passed my house. I waved at Latrine. We locked eyes again. I started to cry. Mimi approached me. Mimi treated me different than the rest of her grandkids. I suppose she knew that I needed more love than the rest of them. They all had normal mothers, and mine was a violent raging alcoholic.

"I love you, Enola." She said.

"I love you to Mimi." I hugged her. It was a rare occasion that I hugged Mimi or she told me she loved me. She was an amazing woman, but one that showed very little physical affection. My father and grandfather were this way too. I naturally had become this way. The only person that ever touched me and told me they loved me had brutally raped me for seven years in a row. Was it suddenly over? I longed for the day Latrine would leave grandma's house. It would all end, and things would be normal again, but what was normal? He had raped me since I was so young, I didn't remember life without Latrine sexually abusing me. It had become my normal. I lived a double life, before my age reached double digits.

The phone rang.

"Hello." Mimi answered it. "Yes, one moment please." She nudged me and handed me the phone.

"Hello?" I was leery, I didn't know who was on the other end.

"Enola, it's me Alex."

"Alex! I am so sorry about your dad." I was so glad to hear back from him.

"Enola, I need you to tell on Latrine. Today." Alex demanded.

"Tell on him for what, Alex?" I asked.

Was my secret not a secret with Alex? Did he actually know, or is he fishing?

"Enola, I know he touches you." Alex responded.

"Ok, well do you want me to call you later Alex?" I didn't want to ask him what he was talking about in front of Mimi.

"No Enola, he almost killed my dad, I want you to tell." Alex said.

"How do you know he did, not about your dad, the other thing?" I interrogated Alex a little.

"I know because Doug told me, a few years ago." Alex said.

So now Alex knows too. I'm so embarrassed. I want to hang this phone up and end my life. Everyone is going to hate me. I'm so over with. What if the whole neighborhood has seen the tape Doug has. Oh my god.

"My mom is in Vegas. I will when she gets home." I responded.

"It's not your fault you know." Alex said.

"Come and get me when you get out of the shower, so we can walk and talk."

"I can't. I'm not allowed to hang out with you anymore now Enola, my dad said you are Latrine's family, and you can't mean well. You have to tell on Latrine, Enola." Alex sounded like he might cry.

"Goodbye Alex." I hung the phone up. Little did I know, that was the last time I would ever speak to Alex again. He went away to a mental institution the next week. I was deeply hurt by losing Alex. The summer before I followed him to the nearest main road, walking. He didn't know I was behind him. He walked out into the road and laid down. I ran out and laid beside him. I told him if he was going, I was too. I knew I would never forget Alex, so long as I lived.

CHAPTER 10 TWO KIDS PLAYING

"If you would keep ya ass out of a bar and at home, she wouldn't be saying those things. Cassidy Lynn, they are kids. If anything happened, they were surely playing." My grandmother had just started with the series of insults. "Enola is a liar, I thought it and now I know it."

"I won't sit here and listen to this." My mother responded.

"If you plan on escalating this outside of these four walls, you aren't really welcome too." My grandmother had not one ounce of sympathy for the news my mother had just delivered. Unbeknown to my mother at the time, this was not brand-new information to my grandmother.

"Mom-" My mother attempted to get a word in.

"Cassidy, Enola wants her mom's attention. Nothing more." My grandmother repeated the hurtful things she had already said.

"Mom- If Enola is lying, how does she know you own a white dildo?" I was mortified that my mother would disclose the details I had just shared with her moments earlier.

"I- What?" My grandmother's face turned red.

"Yeah, your white dildo from your side table, Mom he used it on Enola. Sick fuck." My mother had changed and raised the tone of her voice.

"I don't own one of those." My grandmother insisted.

All my mother's siblings lived with my grandmother at the time, and they were all present for the conversation.

"Yes, you do Mom. Let's go look." My mother took it there.

"Get the fuck out of here Cassidy." My aunt entered the conversation.

"Who asked you Bozo?" My mother fired back.

"Nobody asked me, but I'm fixin' to come up off this couch and whoop your ass."

Bozo was a fighter. I suppose we all were. Grandma had instilled it into all of us from a young age. Grandma's house had lots of violence hiding behind those seemingly welcoming doors.

"Bozo are you mad because nobody stuck up for you?" My mother knew no boundaries. "Do you wish mom had held Uncle JJ responsible when he raped you for so many years? Do you?"

My mother had started to act out. I still could not see her, but I could hear her. I was still on the front porch, alone. I had back against the house, opposite the picture window, hoping to remain unnoticed.

"Cassidy, do you have to?" My grandfather had finally spoke up.

"Are you siding with the little fat fucker too, Dad?" My mother was hurt.

"I'm not siding with anyone, but I'm with your mama, what if they was only two damned kids playing? Kids get do shit Cassidy."

I couldn't believe the words I was hearing my grandparents speak. My grandmother had caught my uncle Latrine on several occasions, touching my innocent young body. She had even disclosed once to Papal when Papal beat the cards out of Latrine's hands years earlier. They knew. How could they be talking about me this way? My heart was heavy. I was second guessing my decision to tell my mother now.

"She was five, Dad." My mother cried.

"We have to talk to Latrine, you don't know that, Cassidy."

"Are you calling Enola a liar, Dad?"

"No, Cassidy."

"It sounded to me like you just called my daughter a liar."

"I'm just saying we need to make sure what she is saying is true."

"And you think Latrine will just admit it? Good fucking grief, are you all fucking dumb Dad?"

"Cass-" My grandfather laid his hand on my mother's shoulder attempting to calm her down.

"No, don't fucking Cass me. I've let a lot go, Dad, this, I can and will not." My mother took a deep breath. "I'm going to the prison tomorrow to confront this fucker myself, Dad."

"The phone should be ringing anytime." My grandfather said.

"Yeah, and she or her little lying ass daughter are speaking to him. Latrine is in prison having a hard enough time as it is, we aren't adding to that." My grandmother overrode my grandfather.

Sure enough she had seen me. Before anyone could approach me outside of the window the telephone rang.

"Corrections state of Ohio, there the son of a bitch is now." My mother lunged for the phone.

My grandmother battled her for it, but my mother wasn't letting go. Not a chance.

"Hey fucker, you got anything to tell me?" My mother answered the phone.

She never was nice to Latrine. I had witnessed her firsthand physically abuse Latrine several times in my life. He used to panic at the sight of her, I couldn't imagine how he felt hearing her like that.

"What do you mean?"

"Don't play dumb Latrine. I'm coming there tomorrow to confront you in front of all the inmates. I don't care. They will do to you, what you did."

"Enola?"

"Latrine, yes, tell mom what you did to Enola."

"Not on this line."

Did he just? What? Did he just admit to what he has done? No. Couldn't be.

"So you aren't calling her a liar, Latrine?" My mother badgered.

"No, I would never call Enola a liar, Cassidy."

"Latrine- Keep your god damned mouth shut." My grandmother invaded.

"Latrine you will stay away from my daughter, for the rest of her life, do you hear me?" My mother scolded Latrine through the phone.

Latrine was obviously crying. I could hear every detail; she had the speaker phone on.

"Cassidy-" Latrine attempted to interrupt my mother.

My grandmother jerked the phone out of my mother's hand.

"Fuck you, Mom." My mother went there, again.

"Mom," I grabbed her arm as she stormed out the front door.

"Enola, I am sorry."

"Are you ok Mom?"

My grandmother kicked her screen door open. It hit the house. My mother shielded my head and started to walk faster down the driveway towards the street. I still don't know what she was shielding me from.

"Don't you come back here, Cassidy Lynn. You or your lying ass daughter. Give her some attention, why don't you?" My grandmother screamed at my mother from the porch.

"Yeah, don't blame your child molester of a son." My mother yelled back. She gripped my hand even tighter. She walked faster and faster until we reached our front door.

"I still want to see Papal." I quietly spoke.

"You will one day, he will get over it. Papal is not angry, he is hurt. Hurt causes us to act out angry sometimes, Enola."

I laid down on the couch with my face into the cushions. I could no longer hide my tears and I did not want my mother to see them.

"It's ok to cry, Enola." My mother rubbed my back.

My mother rarely showed me any physical affection. The feeling of her French manicured acrylics, caressing my back, was one I had not often felt.

I fell asleep that night with the feeling of the love I had imagined feeling for so many years before. I felt love from my mother, and it felt amazing. I had only missed what I had imagined, and this was just a piece

47

of it. I don't recall her showing me sympathy beyond that day.

CHAPTER 11 NO SAFE PLACE

I had been in my bedroom for days. I wanted out. I couldn't even believe my mother had stayed home for so many consecutive days. I wanted my father. The events that had landed me confined to my bedroom were ones my father wouldn't discuss with me. I realize now that he silently understood and didn't discipline me for them. I was fourteen years old, and I felt like I knew everything. I was not permitted to have boundaries. My mother made them, and crossed them, while she allowed others to cross them with her. Disrespecting me was only off limits if you disrespected my mother in the process of doing so.

My mother had recently started working third shift. Rather than allowing my brother and I to spend the nights she was working at my father's that week, she hired a babysitter for us. The babysitter was my best friends, older sister, Celeste. My brother was nine years old. My mother didn't trust me with my brother alone because a few years prior I had run away during the night while she worked and left him unattended.

The first night Celeste was over, she invited her boyfriend too. He was just getting ready to head back to college soon. She wanted to spend as much time as she could with him before they went their separate ways.

It wasn't any time before I found myself in yet another awful situation, in a place that should have been my safety grounds, my own home. In fact, it was only the first night when Celeste's boyfriend had awakened me in the middle of the night. Celeste slept next to me. I silently laid awake. He was straddling me and had begun rubbing my back, as I was face down on my couch. I laid there, and to say I rejected his advances would be a lie. I could not believe this was happening to me. I felt special and gross at the same time. Celeste was the girl that everyone wanted, and here her boyfriend was, touching on me. I had been sexually assaulted by Latrine since I was five years old. What I deemed as normal, other girls my age didn't. I allowed her boyfriend to slide my pajama bottoms off and touch me. He was twenty years old. I did not touch him, and I didn't fight him off either. I just allowed him to do whatever he wanted to me.

"Enola are you a virgin?" he suddenly was looking at blood on his fingers.

"No." I responded. I was so confused, as I hadn't looked back, I honestly thought he was having sex with me.

Was I a virgin? I had not consented to sex with a single person yet. I never consented to lose my virginity, but I knew it was gone.

"What just happened?" He asked.

I had felt as if something tore. He had been roughly penetrating me with his fingers. I had frozen, still face down on my own couch, in my own living room.

"Don't tell Celeste, please, Enola." He sounded so pathetic, "This shouldn't have happened, you appear so much older than what you are."

"I won't" I responded. Once again, I had agreed to protect another grown man that hurt me.

"I'll be back tonight, maybe you should stay upstairs." He replied.

I got up and went upstairs to my bedroom. I locked the door behind me, and double checked to make sure that it was locked. I laid down on my bed and felt sick. I knew my mother would blame me for this. I knew I had messed up, big time by allowing him to do the things that he had done. I should have said no. I stared into the dark. I had been grounded to my room for weeks and my mother had removed my television. I was sleeping downstairs with Celeste so that I didn't have to sleep in silence. I couldn't hardly sleep without the television; I had always had one in my bedroom growing up. Jonathon was right, maybe I should stay upstairs and sit within the four walls of my bedroom, exactly where my mother wanted me.

The next morning, I packed my backpack full of clothes and left for school. I had a plan on not returning home that night, but I had no idea where I was going. I had just entered eighth grade, in a school where I had already been bullied for being sexually abused as a child. There was even a rumor that I was dating my uncle and consensually having sex with him. The girl behind the rumor swore my mother started it when I finally confronted her. I never knew if she was fueling my want to end my life, or if it had happened, that my mother was behind this. I hated school. The hallways felt empty, and nothing was fulfilling to me. Life sucked for me.

Celeste's family lived just a few houses down from mine. Her mother Marcia and mine were good friends. Her sister got on the bus right after I did. I avoided eye contact with her. She didn't seem suspicious.

"Good morning, Enola. You look pretty today." She acknowledged me anyways.

"Thanks Ellen." I responded. She had no idea what had unfolded the night before. She was innocent in the situation. I felt fearful around her that morning.

"How you likin' Celeste being your…" she paused and started to whisper, "babysitter?" She finished quietly so nobody else hear her. Afterall, what kind of fourteen-year-old needed a babysitter?

"I don't like Jonathon." I answered. Celeste and her entire family thought the world of Jonathon. I was just the scum with divorced parents down the street.

"Really?" Ellen was shocked.

"Really." I replied.

The bus ride to school went fast that morning, but the day lingered on. I kept checking the time. I started at eight hours until run away time, and finally, two forty-five was here. During the day I plotted out my escape. My best guy friend, Bryan, was picking up a teammate from the middle school every day. I was going to catch a ride back to the high school with him and wait in his car for practice to end. I saw Bryan pull up.

"Hey." I had run to Bryan's window. I was out of breath. "Mom forgot me; will you give me a ride home? I'll wait until your practice is over."

"Get in." He said. Bryan knew the truth behind my tears. He had been an eyewitness to my mother abusing me many, many times. "I know Cassidy didn't forget your ass, what did you do now?" Bryan joked.

"Tell you when we're alone." I laughed and winked at him in the mirror, where the other passenger in the car could not see me.

Bryan was one of the very few male figures in my life that I trusted. I had known him for a long time. My father briefly lived in an apartment complex and Bryan was his neighbor. My mother hated Bryan. She insisted he was too old for me to be hanging out with. He was only two years older than me. Bryan was popular at school, and quite the athlete. His mother was in her sixties. I believe my mother feared Bryan could damage her reputation, because the spotlight was often on him. If he spoke, people might believe him.

We pulled into the school.

"You are literally gonna sit in my car, Enola?" Bryan asked.

"Yes." I answered without hesitation.

"Now that he's gone, what's going on?" Bryan asked.

"Celeste's boyfriend tried to sleep with me last night." I responded. I looked up at Bryan. "He hurt me."

"Enola. Cassidy is going to kill me if she finds you with me. I am not making you go home, but you can't stay with me. Figure out what you're doing." Bryan seemed annoyed I had involved him in harboring a fugitive, that's what I was by now. My mother had surely reported me missing, the second I didn't get off the school bus. "Did you tell her?" Bryan asked.

"No, you know she will kill me." I replied.

Bryan grabbed his bag and thew it over his shoulder, "I'll be back."

I climbed into the front seat and watched all the soccer practice. I

51

was on high alert, as this wasn't my first run away hiatus. I was scanning the parking lot for my mother. An hour and a half felt like eternity. It was finally over. Bryan threw his bags in the trunk and hopped into the car.

"Terrence and Tyrell's Dad's house." Bryan hadn't asked me where I was going, but I told him anyways.

"Do they know?" Bryan asked.

"Yep." I lied. Tyrell would surely hide me; we were great friends. He was a rule breaker, but his twin brother Terrence, was not like us. He would likely be my issue once I got there.

"I'm running home first to shower, you good with it?" Bryan asked.

"Yep." I said.

Maybe once we get there, I can talk you into allowing me to live in your closet for a few days.

We pulled up to Bryan's apartment.

"Duck, Enola." Bryan pushed my head down.

"Shit, why?" I asked.

"Your dad is at my door, there's no way I can stop… he looks super pissed, Enola. Why don't you tell him?" Bryan was attempting to persuade me into doing the right thing. "He will help you, Enola."

"No, drive." I knew my father loved me, and I knew he loved me so much more than my mother did, but she had a way of turning him against me too. "Take me to Tyrell's."

Tyrell lived only a few miles away. Bryan took me there. He didn't even pull in the driveway. He knew my mom was probably hot on my trail, and he didn't want to be a part of it. Bryan had a lot going for him and knew my mother would jeopardize it all if she could.

"Be safe, Enola. Call my house private when you're able." Bryan hugged me before I got out of the car.

"Love you, Bryan." I responded.

"Love you too, Enola."

Bryan drove off, rather quickly. Tyrell had the garage door open when I arrived. As if he knew I would somehow end up there. His bedroom was in the basement. The basement was under his garage, and not his house. A private stairway from the garage led you to the bedroom. I went in, shut the garage door, and headed down the stairs.

"Your mama was here." Tyrell said. "Terrence scared, he told her you were on your way."

"No. Should I leave?" I panicked,

"Nah, I fake like I called you at Bryan's and told you to stay put and act like you agreed. Real G shit baby." Tyrell responded.

I sighed and felt temporarily relieved.

Please don't snitch Bryan. PLEASE, don't snitch.

ENOLA

"Terrence ain't see you come in, be quiet."

"Thank you. I'm so scared." I began to tell Tyrell in graphic details what had happened at my home the night before while my mother worked.

"Jonathon Haynes?" Tyrell asked.

"Yup."

"He done been graduated, Enola, he is grown as hell." Tyrell acknowledged Jonathon's wrongdoing.

I laid down on the futon, that was normally loaded full of teenage boys playing video games. I was exhausted. I knew that my time away would be short lived. I began to cry. Tyrell sat on his bed playing the video game.

"What was that?" I sat up quickly to what sounded like a car hitting Tyrell's garage door.

"I'm gonna find out." Tyrell ran up the stairs.

I heard the garage door open. My mother must have crawled under the door before it was even open.

"Where is the little whore?" My mother was pissed, I could hear it in her voice. I knew for sure, I was in immediate danger.

"She is not here." Tyrell insisted.

My mother went into a fit of rage, the type of fit she usually reserved solely for me behind closed doors. It was the type of fit; I knew I'd be lucky to walk away from uninjured.

"She is here." My mother mocked Tyrell.

"She is not." Tyrell stood strong. "Don't touch me, lady. I'm not your daughter and I'll hit you back." Tyrell's tone had changed.

My mother was a violent human by nature.

"I'm not kidding you, get out of my face." Tyrell demanded her once again.

My mother began calling Tyrell a racial slur, repeatedly. Tyrell kept his cool and didn't respond to the ignorant words my mother was speaking. I could hear her, loud and clear and I couldn't stand to hear what she was saying. I believe she knew exactly how to draw me outside. I took a deep breath and decided to end this for Tyrell. Nobody deserved to endure that. I headed up the stairs.

Suddenly my mother looked past Tyrell, "There the little whore is." She said. "You couldn't even keep your hands of Celeste's boyfriend?" My mother immediately started attacking me. I looked back at Tyrell, somethings didn't need to be spoken, told you so. He looked down and shook his head.

"He raped me." I broke down in tears. My father was present but had returned to the car when my mother started making threats and using the racial slurs.

My mother slapped me in the back of the head so hard, I felt like I was going to throw up. I grabbed the back of my head.

"Act like that hurt, and I'll really hurt you." She had her teeth gritted together. "Get in the fucking car, Enola." My mother demanded.

"Ok." I headed toward the car where I made eye contact with my father. I decided I wasn't ready to go down without a fight. I took off running once I got to my mother's car. She chased me and tackled me to the ground. She punched me in my face several times and dragged me to the car.

"I called the cops, Enola." Tyrell yelled.

Thank you, Jesus. Thank you for the cops being called. I hope they take me away from my mother. I never want to go to my mother's house again!!

"Now you did it. Tell the cops how you slept with your babysitter's boyfriend and now you're calling it rape to ruin his life." My mother spoke the cruelest of words to me.

"I didn't." I got into the car. I figured the sheriff would be at my house. I gave up.

"You did." She said before she got into the car.

My mother picked her car phone up and called the police.

"Yes, I need an officer to meet me at my house with my daughter. She's suicidal and mental and she has hit me." My mother was lying right through her teeth. Dad and I both knew it. "Also, I need to file a report about a twenty-year-old man having a sexual relationship with my daughter as well. Thanks."

"Can't she just go home with me, Cassidy?" My father asked as my mother put her phone back down. "She's been through enough with Latrine, and your family. She doesn't need this shit.

My father rarely braved the storm but today he did. He had seen a full glimpse of my mother in action. She had beat me, the same way she violently beat others while she drank, except she did it sober, because she didn't have to be drunk to hate me. She openly hated me.

"No, you are teaching her to defy me, as her mother." My mother responded. Once again it was all about Cassidy.

"Not everything is about you." My father fired back. "She's never ran away from my house."

My mother became infuriated.

"She's going to fucking jail, just so I know you aren't babying her." My mother began on a rant. "She sleeps around and it's my brother's fault. She back talks me, and it's my brother's fault. She dyes her hair black, and it's my brother's fault."

"Yes, it is, he molested her." My father defended me further. I wanted

54

to correct him and let him know he had in fact, raped me, many times. I knew the difference and my mother still refused to call it what it was. That large detail kept Latrine safely out of prison.

"So, let's baby her and let her turn into a crack head with six baby daddies. She enticed Celeste's boyfriend. He said she came on to him, what don't you understand about this situation?"

We pulled up to the home. There was a female detective at my door already. Word traveled fast that a twenty-year-old man had touched me. My mother sent me upstairs as soon as we got home. I watched a crime scene van pull into my mother's driveway. They came in and took my mother's couch cushions where the incident had just occurred. The detective took me down to the police station and took a statement. I told her how horrible my mother had been to me. I knew she believed me. I know now, she legally wasn't permitted to send me home with my Mimi, but she did that night anyways. The department charged me with domestic violence because I had hit my mother back. The detective told Mimi to keep me until my court date would occur. Two days later, Mimi brought me back to that building for court. My mother insisted jail time would be in my best interest, that I needed tough love. Despite the rape investigation surrounding my bizarre behavior, the judge sent me to the juvenile detention center. I got out a few days later, and Jonathon was arrested on felony charges for sexually assaulting me.

"Celeste is coming over here. She wants and deserves answers." My mother opened my bedroom door, no sooner than I shut it. "And you're going to give them to her, Enola."

I didn't want any of this to happen. This is a nightmare. I don't want to see Celeste.

"Ok." I agreed. I could read my mother's moods. She had been drinking a little heavier than normal lately. I noticed it; despite her attempts to hide it, and constant claims that she had not drank in x number of days. I feared her the most when she was drunk.

"She's coming now, Enola."

"Ok." I responded with my head down.

"Lift your head up Enola, for fuck's sake this isn't about you." My mother said.

"Ok." I lifted my head up.

Celeste came shortly after. She interrogated me like a serial killer that was potentially facing the death penalty. The hate in her eyes wouldn't let a tear expose itself. She was bold, she was mad, and she wanted revenge. I wouldn't give Celeste much attention. My purple sponged walls had become the four walls of an interrogation room. She was even permitted to shut and lock the door behind her. Celeste kept on telling me she couldn't believe I had done this to her. She yelled, she cried, and she hugged. Her emotions were all over the place. She kept asking me why. I didn't have an answer for her. I was guilty of only sleeping outside of my bedroom. She got up to leave my bedroom after one hour and forty give minutes. She turned toward me at the opened door.

"Enola, one last thing?" Celeste asked.

I glared at her, "Yeah?"

"You told me you weren't a virgin, but Jonathon said he popped your cherry, why did you lie?"

She never took her eyes off me. The room felt cold and empty. I stared back at her. I couldn't believe the nasty question she had just asked me. I didn't even know what a cherry was.

"You don't know?" I responded.

Our families had been close friends for years. We played on sports teams together, we were on the same swim team and my dad had coached us for many years. I had assumed my mother shared great details of my abuse from Latrine with Celeste's mother.

"Know what?" Celeste asked.

"My uncle Latrine raped me. My whole childhood." I responded.

"Oh, now everyone rapes you, Enola?" Celeste shut the door.

The joke was definitely on Celeste. Jonathon served five years community patrol. He was kicked out of college and forced to stay away from children for a duration of ten years. My mother pushed for the maximum penalties, and she also received the maximum amount of restitution in the case. I watched my mother ruin Jonathon from start to finish. I only wish she had done the same to Latrine.

CHAPTER 12 EASTER IN THE ICU

It was an Easter Sunday that I will never forget. I had anxiously arrived at the hospital. I had received news no child should ever receive. My mother had attempted suicide and the fate of her survival was unknown. Mimi had called around town to reach me that morning. I was only fourteen. I had snuck out of Mimi's house the night before with my much older boyfriend, Melvin.

Melvin had an extremely odd attachment to my mother that I was unable to recognize as young woman. I thought she was the mother he had always needed. He held my hand as we entered the cold, quiet hospital room. Melvin closed the door behind him.

"Oh my god, Cassidy." Melvin sighed at the sight of my mother.

He was much more hurt than I was about it. Not to say seeing my mother that way didn't break me, but at that moment I did not feel a thing. This woman had beaten me up like a grown woman she was fighting in a bar. Mimi had recently stopped by and caught her dragging me to my bedroom by my hair for a beating. She had, had me incarcerated the Easter before for not wearing a pair of pants she picked out for me. I had begged my mother to allow me to move in with my father. In the days prior to her attempt, she had expressed to me that I was pushing her over the edge, because I didn't want to go home. I didn't want to go home because she drank excessively and insulted me, all hours of the night, into the morning often. My friends weren't allowed at her house because of the things she had done in front of them while drinking. I could not live a normal life while living with my mother full time. It was comparable to what you would picture World War three to be.

"This is your fault, Enola."

"Darrian, are you kidding me?" I responded.

Darrian was my mother's only true friend. He and her had so much in common. The two things that stood out, they were both alcoholics, and they were both selfish. I hated Darrian

"You are a spoiled brat...you should've come home- Now you don't have the chance." Darrian's words cut like a knife.

"This really is your fault, Enola." My mother's coworker added her two cents.

"Fuck you, Katrina." I grabbed Melvin and attempted to exit the room.

The phone rang, connected to my mother's bed, where her lifeless body lied. My mind wondered, who that would be. I walked back into the room and looked at everyone before I picked the phone up.

"Hello."

"Enola, where's Cassidy?"

It was my mother's friend, Marcia. Marcia was my babysitter Celeste's mother. She deeply cared for us, and despite her sometimes-odd way of showing it, I knew it.

"She, uh… can't talk."

"Enola, what is going on?" Marcia was worried.

"Mom tried to kill herself." I whispered.

"What, Enola?" Marcia was in shock.

"Yeah. And Darrian and Katrina said it's my fault." My voice quivered.

"Enola, I will be there in a minute, go out in the lobby."

"Okay." I agreed.

"Promise, Enola?" Marcia made sure I was leaving that room full of idiots.

"I promise."

I hung hit the red button on the phone to end our conversation. I untangled the phone cord from the bed. Afterall, my mother would not be using it anytime soon. I grabbed my bag and exited the room alone. Nobody followed me, not even Melvin. Somehow, I always ended up alone when I needed someone the most. My mother always got all the attention, by any account.

I sat in the empty lobby for what felt like hours that day. I watched as the visitors for my mother came and went. I had a pit in my stomach thinking about how Bubba was going to handle my mother's obvious coming death. I always worried about Bubba.

I looked up and seen my father. It was then I realized that Marcia had called my father and told him everything I had just told her. He had come to save me, once again.

"Enola, honey!!" My father was relieved to had laid eyes on me.

"Daddy, I don't want mom to die." My voice was monotone.

"She won't. She will fight and she will live." My father hugged me.

"Darrian told me she did this because of me, and Katrina-"

"What?"

"Yeah, I didn't mean to make her want to die, Dad." I felt the tears as I accepted the responsibility Darrian and Katrina had wrongfully placed on me.

"Enola, you didn't. I am going to get you home." My father grabbed me and led me out behind him.

My father's face was pale white, as if he had seen a ghost. Nobody loved my mother more than my father did, except maybe Papal. My father was physically sick over what had occurred. The ride home was silent, until we neared the house.

ENOLA

"Enola... Bubba is little, we need to keep this from him." My father said.

"I don't want him to know either. He hasn't seen the bad in her, Dad." I responded.

"There is no bad in your mother Enola, she doesn't know what it's like to be happy. I hope she gets help." My father wiped his eyes.

"If she makes it, Dad." I responded.

"She will." He never spoke another word on the rest of the drive home.

I wiped my tears and calmed myself. Bubba would not know anything was off unless we told him. We stayed with Dad for days on end before she showed up to take us for a fun outing anyways, only to bring us back the following day so she could go drink.

I observed the sidewalk beneath my feet. I had walked down this sidewalk as a small girl. I had run down this sidewalk after Latrine raped me, hundreds of times. I had run down this sidewalk after Alex's dog bit me. I had played hopscotch on this sidewalk; on a course I drew myself. I had walked down this sidewalk home to and with my family, and then only to my mother and her boyfriend, and then back to it only being my father's home. This sidewalk had carried many unsteady footsteps. If this sidewalk could talk, it would have a story to tell. The sidewalk that had caught my tears, for so many years. I now walked down this sidewalk wondering if my mother would survive the night, on Easter Sunday. I walked down this sidewalk, and I prayed.

The next few days would come and go in the blink of an eye. I must have disassociated myself from reality. It was awful at the time. I hadn't seen Melvin since I left the hospital unannounced with my father. I hadn't been back to the hospital either. The day had come they were going to remove the tube from my mother and see if she would wake up. My father didn't think it was a good idea for me to go, but I was going whether he liked it or not, he knew it, so he agreed to stand go with me. He and my mother had been separated for about two years.

I walked into my mother's patient room. The room had a much different feel to it this time. Darrian nor Katrina was there, but Melvin was. He never left. My father hated Melvin. I was fourteen and he was twenty. My mother condoned our relationship, but my father despised it. Rightfully so, I was only a child still. Melvin equally despised of my father and did not even try to act like he respected him.

"Who brought that?" I asked.

There was a six-foot-tall light pink teddy bear sitting in the chair beside my mother's bed.

"I did." Melvin grinned. "Do you like it, Enola?"

"It's cute." I responded.

"It's damn weird." My father said.

I sat down opposite the bear beside my mother's bed. I caressed her arm, just as she had mine years prior when I told her what Latrine did to me. I looked at my mother and was suddenly lost in my thoughts. I glared out the window past my mother. There she was, baby squirrel, running across the drying roof of the hospital. The sun was shining after a light rain. My grandmother was good for a few lessons in life. She always told me when it rained like that and the sun shined, God was crying but he was ok. I knew I would be too that day. Baby squirrel ran in and out of the puddles on the roof. She hoped up on the side and I lost sight of her. Baby squirrel reminded me of the battles my mother and I had endured together. I shifted my focus back onto my mother. I needed her and I knew it. It wasn't until later, I realized again, the woman I needed, was just a mere figment of my imagination. She never did exist. I still dreamt of it though, prayed for it, rather.

I stood up and moved my mother's matted curls behind her ears out of her face. I stared at her lifeless face and remembered the pain she had also endured. My mother was also raised in a family of secrets. My grandparents had swept countless cases of sexual abuse under the rug. My aunt, my uncle, and now me. Was my mother also a victim of this vicious cycle? My mind was racing a mile a minute. I was young, I was curious, and I was suddenly determined to deep dive into my mother's mind. She was a woman of many, many secrets.

"Enola!" My father nudged me.

"What" I shook my head.

"I've said your name three times. Are you ok?" My father was concerned.

"Yeah, sorry."

"Hi Enola, we are going to wake your mother up. We would like for you all to step out into the waiting area while we remove the breathing tube.

"Ok." I obliged.

We all exited the room into the hallway. I had been holding in many secrets about Melvin, that I couldn't tell, because I had agreed to things with him before. Nobody would believe me if I told them what he had done to me. I couldn't get rid of Melvin. Weeks prior Melvin had raced past my mother's home while he told me to look out the window and that he was going to end his life. My mother had talked him out of it, but still allowed him at the house. It was a nightmare I had convinced myself I was enjoying. I stood next to my father. Melvin stood beside me.

"Alright, you can come back in." The doctor came back after only a few minutes.

We entered the room. There was a nurse beside my mother. They had brought in a dry erase board for my mother to communicate with if she woke up normal. The doctor had explained she wouldn't be able to talk because of the amount of time the tube was in her throat. My mother slowly woke up. She observed the room for only a few moments before she motioned for the nurse to hand her the dry erase board. She grabbed it. It took her quite a while to write the four words she wrote. She turned the dry erase board around.

"I love you, Melvin." I read the board out loud.

"I love you too, Cassidy." Melvin knelt and hugged my mother.

"I love you Mom." I said.

She looked up at me. She did not write anything to me on her board. The look in her eyes, despite the look of exhaustion, was still a look of disgust. I could not believe it. She was blaming me too, and I could feel it, as if I had forced her to do what she had done to land her where she was at. It was always somehow my fault, even this.

CHAPTER 13 ZERO 1 SIX EIGHT ZERO

"Zero-One-Zero-Six-Eight-Zero" I gave the nurse my temporary Identification number. My mother did not find the humor in me referring to myself as a series of numbers, nor as my psych ID, my temporary ID. "Do I really need all of these?" I offered a bit of resistance to swallowing the contents inside the small white paper cup.

"If you want to go home, you do." The nurse rebutted.

"So, if I don't take these..." I couldn't believe the words she had just spoke. I was legally a child still, but at this point in my life, my thought process mimicked and surpassed that of most grown women. My father told my mother earlier that day that I would manipulate the doctor into allowing me to leave the hospital. I knew my mother had manipulated him to believe I was sick. He makes jokes about me getting out of the three-day mandatory hold early. He called me a master manipulator back then, but really the doctor seen right through my unstable, alcoholic mother. My father was the one being master manipulated. I always felt bad for his inability to see through my mother. "I don't get to go home? So, I am being forced, to take these?" I responded.

"Enola, what's your last name and date of birth?" she ran straight past the question I had just asked her.

"I don't get to go home unless I take these?" I asked again.

"I'm going to see if the Doctor is in, Enola, I'm not doing this with you today." She walked away rather disgusted. She turned back to lock her med cart. "This is all unnecessary. You aren't leaving here early."

"Alright Cheryl." I responded.

"She's refusing them." Cheryl was headed back down the hallway with the Doctor. I hadn't met him. There was a new doctor every day. I was in an adult/youth blended psychiatric unit. The small town I live in did not and still doesn't offer a children's unit.

"Hi, I'm Enola." I looked at the nurse who had just asked me to confirm the details of my identity, beyond the eight-digit temporary one they given me. "Enola Wilson." I offered the doctor my first and last name. "I'm over medicated and I need to live with my dad or my grandmother." I knew the odds of my mother agreeing to let my father have me were slim. The chance of Mimi demanding me return to her house, my safe place was high as well.

"Come talk with me, Enola." The doctor gently tapped my shoulder.

ENOLA

"Do you want her pills?" The nurse followed up.

"No, not right now, it's not necessary." The doctor quickly deescalated the quickly rising situation.

My mother was not permitted to watch my every move. She was only allowed in during the hospital's visitation hours, and only if I permitted her. I felt safe, safe enough to semi tell my truth for the first time. Although it was a mere piece of it, I felt empowered sharing it.

"I'm not crazy, and I didn't try to kill myself." I explained.

The doctor picked up a manilla folder with my name on the tag in red permanent marker. Wilson, Enola. He licked his finger like doctors do, and began shuffling though the pages, one by one. He was very obviously summarizing himself to familiarity with my file.

"So, Enola, if you didn't want to end your life, why did you take all of your prescriptions? Sixty pills, Enola?" He asked me.

"I want out of my mother's. I can't take it anymore." I responded, with complete and utter honesty. "She is an alcoholic. She abuses me. She allows other people to abuse me." I rambled on.

"Enola, what is your mother's favorite color?" He asked.

The question caught be my surprise. "Her favorite color? I don't know." I answered.

"Enola, if you could be anywhere in the world right now, where would you be?" He asked.

"At my aunt's house, swimming with my cousins. She had an inground pool. Mimi takes me and my brother there often." I responded.

"So you like to swim at your aunts?" He was writing in a notebook.

"Yes. I love my aunt's house." I responded.

Mimi and my aunt were the best of friends. They did everything together, and that didn't change when I was born, they just allowed me to come too. I was a part of a family with Mimi, my dad and his amazing siblings. Mimi raised kind humans, much opposite of the humans my grandmother had reproduced.

"Are you safe with your Dad?" He asked.

"My Daddy is my best friend. Mom keeps him mad at me. No matter what I say, she turns him against me. Dad has been sad since he left Mom." I responded.

"Has anyone hurt you since you have been here, Enola?"

Why is he asking me all these bizarre questions? I just want to go home to my dad's. Please help me.

"Downstairs when I first got here. After I took the pills. My mom hurt me." I looked up at the Doctor across the desk. I had his full attention, and I knew it. "She grabbed my hair and pulled my head backwards and dumped the drink in my mouth. The drink to make me puke. I was having a hard time swallowing it. It—"

"It's nasty, so nasty you could barely drink it?" He finished my sentence.

"Yes, I gagged, and she hurt my head when she pulled my hair. She's been pulling my hair since I was nine years old." I had never confessed that to anyone. "Mimi seen her once, she came by the house to pick me up and my mother was furious at me for something. She was dragging me, my feet dragging too, from the kitchen to my bedroom, which was approximately 50 feet." I took a deep breath. I could feel the tears fighting to fall. I had been holding them back so strong. I had grown to hold everything in.

"Here, Enola." The doctor handed me a tissue. "Take a deep breath."

I did. I exhaled. "She's mean and nobody believes me." I wiped my eyes by the corner with the tissue, attempting not to smear my white drawn on eye shadow.

"I believe you, Enola." He responded.

I kept my guard up with all men, even this doctor. In my mind I was questioning his intentions even, but I continued anyways. "A few weeks ago, I ran away from home. Mom took a bottle of sleeping pills and drank a fifth of vodka." I wiped my tears further. "A friend of hers stopped by when she quit texting back. He found her on the floor, lifeless. They told me all about it. When I got to the hospital, they told me this had all happened because of me." I had never spoke my full truth to anyone before that moment.

My teacher and mentor had visited me in the emergency room. He reminded me none of the things that happened to me were my fault. He encouraged me to be the best version of myself, the young lady he knew I could be, in his words. He told me to tell the truth and he would see me at school every day to confirm I was safe, and if I wasn't he would personally keep me at the school, until child protective services took me to safety. He had silently observed her from a distance for the past year. She missed every game I was a cheerleader in. This was noticed at the small catholic school she sent me to. Her mischievous behavior wasn't accepted, and my new peers and their parents weren't welcoming of her the rare occasion she did show up. I knew Roy would never misguide me. I heard every word he had spoken, and I believed him. I spoke my truth because he gave me the courage to do so.

"You know, Enola, the actions of others aren't your fault. Especially the adults in your life. I think you are a courageous young girl. I am going to encourage the courts to enforce family counseling. I'm also recommending from a medical perspective that you are discharged with your father. I can't enforce this though, Enola. It's solely a recommendation." This doctor was more like an angel in disguise. He was my steppingstone out of what I had deemed the garden of hell. "I see no reason to hold you for an additional forty-eight hours and I'd like to disregard any potential changes we were making to your medication." He was writing all of what he was telling me down on his notepad.

I got up from the chair and headed back to my room. I was sharing the room with another female, close to my age. She had been sexually assaulted by her basketball coach. I had explained to her earlier that morning that I was going to get out of that place, that day.

"I'm leaving." I said as I entered the room.

"You dirty ass dog, doing me like that," She joked.

"I am writing my number down and I want you to call me when you get out, girl." I said.

"No doubt baby." She hugged me. I could feel the loneliness vibing right out of her soul.

"Don't hurt yourself, I need a friend." I smirked. I was serious though.

"I won't. You gave me strength, Enola." She hugged me again.

I gathered my things and headed for the lobby. I knew the doctor had called my parents to explain the discharge recommendations. I just didn't know which parent was coming to get me. I had hoped it was my father. In fact, I had not considered my mother showing up to get me. I had presumed she would follow the doctor's recommendation. I was stressed, and only a human. I deserved that peace. I laid down on the leather couch in the lobby. The door buzzed every few minutes. I kept looking up. There was no sign of my father. It felt as if hours had gone by, it was only minutes. I picked a magazine up from the table and began to read. I stopped paying attention to the door. I was patiently waiting.

"Hey Enola." The voice of my mother sent chills down my spine.

"Hey." I know she heard the disappoint in my voice.

"You're not throwing fits and getting your way. Not on my watch." She immediately started her drama with me. We hadn't even left the floor that I was supposed to be confined to for the next two days.

"Ok." I quietly responded. I was embarrassed she was treating me this way in front of another patient. I looked up and her. She nodded her head.

"Don't say shit and come on, Enola." My mother grabbed my arm. She had a secret tight hold on me. She squeezed me as we passed the nurse's station. She silently told me to remain silent. She could speak to me without speaking at all. I feared her. She held onto me that way until we reached the car. "Get in, Enola." She opened the door and headed toward her side of the car.

"Am I going to Dad's?" I asked and with no hesitation this time.

Without warning, she slapped me across the face. "How fucking dare, you, Enola."

"So, I'm not?" I antagonized her once I realized she was going to give me a reaction.

"Enola, shut up." My mother had a hold of the steering wheel. She was so mad at me she was shaking from gripping it so tight. "I can't stand you."

"That's no secret." I replied.

"Enola, shut up." She demanded.

I didn't say another word. I stared outside of the window and counted the telephone poles as we passed them. As soon as my mother turned onto her street, I felt cold. There was not an ounce of love for me in that home, and I knew it. I longed for the day I could call my father's house home. He was my safe place, and my desired location to live. We pulled into my mother's garage.

"Go to your fucking room, and don't even think about coming out." My mother demanded.

I went upstairs to my room. I immediately noticed white ruffled curtains were hung on my window the day that I was gone. Big girly ruffled curtains.

"Do you like the curtains?" My mother asked. She entered my bedroom behind me.

"No." I responded.

"You're pretty fucking rude considering the things you have done." She snapped at me.

"I don't like ruffles, but this is your room, not mine." I responded, "I hate it here."

I hadn't even looked at my bed when my mother picked up a pair of blue jeans, she had kept possession of since her sophomore year of high school in 1986. They were distressed wash and the furthest thing from in style. I thought it was odd they were laying there, but I thought nothing of it.

"Do you like these?" My mother picked up the jeans.

"Ew, no." I responded.

"You're wearing them to school tomorrow." She raised her voice slightly.

"No, I'm not." I insisted.

"Yes, you are Enola Denise Wilson." She threw the jeans at me.

I didn't say anything back to my mother. The phone rang. She left the room to answer it. She had disconnected my telephone in my bedroom so I couldn't contact anyone she didn't know about. I picked the jeans up and looked at them. I was already being bullied in school. I knew there was no way I could wear those jeans. I had just started middle school and I would be the laughingstock of lunch. I felt a tear drop down my face. I tried to stop myself from crying, but the thought of going to school in those jeans really upset me.

"It's your dad on the phone. Don't cause any havoc, Enola, or you won't talk to him again." She waved me toward the stairs to the kitchen.

"Hello." I said.

"Enola, you ok honey?" The sound of my father's voice brought an instant feeling of peace over me. I knew he truly cared about my well-being. I knew my mother was jealous.

"No, she's trying to make me wear her old straight leg jeans to school." My mother jerked the phone out of my hand.

"This is exactly why I didn't want you calling today." She hung the phone up on my father.

I do not know how long my mother and I argued back and forth about the jeans that night. She had cooked bratwurst for dinner on top of it. I hated bratwurst. My mother had a rule that if we didn't eat what she cooked, we didn't eat at all. I don't know if she knew it or cared, but I went to bed hungry that night. Bratwurst physically made me ill and I had not eaten breakfast in the hospital that morning. I cried myself to sleep that night.

"Get up." My mother screamed at me.

I never woke up peacefully. I was always awakened by her yelling. She was never calm when approaching us to wake us out of a dead sleep. She instilled anxiety into me from a young age, I always woke up afraid, and in a complete panic.

"I didn't mean to fall asleep, I'm sorry." I offered her an apology. I am not sure now for what.

"Put the jeans on, Enola." She picked up right where she had left off.

"No." I responded.

She grabbed a hold of me and tried to pull my pajama bottoms off me, so that she could dress me, as if I were a small child. She was doing exactly what Latrine had done to me so many times and it was all I could think about.

"Hold still, you're wearing these fucking jeans, rather I have to dress you, or not." She yelled.

"No." I yelled back. I was guarding my face as I saw my mother draw back to hit me. I grabbed her hand after I blocked her hitting me and I twisted her thumb. I heard it snap. I knew I had just broken my own mother's thumb. I felt sick. I never wanted to hurt my mother; despite the times she had hurt me.

"You little brat." She was enraged that I had just broke her thumb. She slapped me. I hit my head on the bed post and she grabbed me to pull be back up. I swung with no aim, but towards my mother's face. I was defending myself as if I were in a fight in the school gymnasium.

"Leave me alone Mom." I screamed so loud, hoping the neighbors would hear. I know they did, and chose to ignore me, as always.

"Put these pants on, Enola." She demanded again.

"No." I screamed at the top of my lungs, to the point my throat hurt. I know now I was reacting to the years of abuse I had endured by numerous people.

"I'm calling the cops on you again, Enola." She slammed my bedroom door and held it shut from the outside. I wanted out. I began hitting the door. My mother had dispatch on the phone. She had turned the speaker on so I could hear them, and maybe so they could hear me.

"Help!" I screamed.

My father was giving me a ride to school that day. Rather than pulling in and picking me up for school, he saw me being dragged to the cop car in handcuffs. I stared at my father as the cop guarded my head to put me into the cruiser. He took the handcuffs off me. I flipped my mother off as she stood on the porch. My father could not believe the behavior I had just displayed. The cop backed out of my mother's driveway. My father was bawling his eyes out. I had never seen a grown man cry so hard. He knew I did not belong in the detention center, again. This was the second time a pair of jeans would land me there.

The next morning an attorney showed up to represent me in juvenile court. His name was John. A staff member had taken me to a small concrete room where I met with him. He explained to me that I had been charged with domestic violence and being unruly. He told me not to say anything and he would handle it. We entered court. The judge accepted the pleas of no contest, entered on my behalf. She sentenced me to ninety days in the detention center and suspended it, forcing me to agree I would not get it anymore trouble. The judge also temporarily placed me with my father, which would naturally become my primary residence, even after the court order expired.

CHAPTER 14 AMANDA

Latrine had not been home from prison any time before he met Amanda. Amanda was a different kind of girl. I loved Amanda. We had something in common. We were both young. Amanda was a rebellious teenager. She came from a nice family. Her father worked in law enforcement and her mother worked for our county. Amanda was a beautiful vibrant soul. I was never sure what it was that she seen in Latrine.

"He had better watch out for that one." Grandma reached up and slugged me. I was sitting beside my cousin Skyla on the couch. Grandma was sitting in between her legs, but on the floor. She had her head facing downward and Skyla had a comb, scratching her head. It was one of Grandma's many disgusting nervous habits, that I refused to take part in. I was never going to be caught dead scratching the dead skin off Grandma's head. Skyla did it four hours, and often. Everyone, but me did.

Neither me nor Skyla responded to Grandma's comment. Latrine and Amanda had barely made it down to the dungeon when she said it.

"Nobody else sees through the little wench?" Grandma followed up.

"I like her." I offered a bold response.

"You're probably jealous of her." My grandmother responded.

I was mortified by the words my grandmother had just spoken. How could she be so cruel? It was always clear my mother forced me back into a family that indeed, wanted no part of me. I didn't want any part of them either. My grandmother's words cut like a knife. I swear she knew how to hurt me worse than anyone else.

"Latrine is a pervert." I choked up after I spoke.

My grandmother lifted herself into a standing position from the ground.

"What did you say?" She asked.

I could tell she was mad. I swallowed the saliva in my mouth.

"Latrine is a pervert. You know it. That's why you don't like Amanda."

"Enola, do not start your shit with this one." My grandmother shook her head. "Like I said, jealous. It shows. You and your mama are just the same."

"Fuck you Grandma." I did not hesitate with that sentence either.

My grandmother had surely crossed a line and I was not willing to stand for it any longer. My grandmother's eyes opened wide. Nobody ever talked back to Grandma.

"I can't believe you just said that to Grandma." Her response. She is where my mother learned to play the victim from. I wasn't having it.

"Fuck you, Grandma." I said it again.

I felt empowered insulting my grandmother even though I knew it was wrong. She could have prevented my abuse. Rather she remained silent and added to it.

"I am done." I added.

"You can be done, you and your mama." She responded. She never insulted me directly, she always included my mother, she still does. Her eyes were blood shot, she had one too many drinks. It was obvious by this point. She was not mean when she was sober, but that very seldomly happened. She walked into the kitchen. "You can leave." She pointed at the door.

"You don't have to tell my twice. I'm out." I got up and walked to the door, where I sat down to put my shoes on. I looked up at Skyla. She looked back at me. We spoke without speaking. I knew she was on my side, but she was too afraid to speak up. Skyla knew more than she wanted me to know she knew.

"I'm telling Cassidy how you have spoken to me, Enola. Ya little bitch." My grandmother was walking towards me at the door. She was certainly a person that thought respect was given and not earned.

I quickly stood up and walked out the front door. I knew my grandmother would not put her hands on me, but I still feared her. I looked back. She was standing at the door. She looked hurt.

"Latrine raped me, and he's raping Amanda too. She's a kid, you know!" I yelled back at my grandmother once I reached the street.

"Bla bla bla Enola. Nobody gives a shit. We all know your mommy is a drunk and you need attention. Latrine did not do anything you did not want him to do. You were two kids playing, nothing more."

She spoke fast but efficient. She also spoke loudly, loud enough for her neighbors, the Carlisle's, to hear from their front porch.

"I'm not lying, and you know it." I was determined to get the last word.

I approached my sidewalk. Our house was the only house on the street with a sidewalk. Once even one of my feet touched the sidewalk, I knew I was almost home. I ran down the sidewalk and into the house. I locked the door behind me. My father was still at his shop working on his car. I had planned to sleep over at my grandmother's. I picked the cordless phone up off the family computer desk. I called my father.

"Dad!"

"Hello- Enola?"

"Dad. Grandma said I was jealous of Amanda." I took a deep breath, "Why does she have to say stuff like that to me?"

"Enola, I have told you. The only way to avoid this pain is to cut those hillbillies out of your life Stop going down there. You have too." He responded.

"Dad it's my family." I became defensive each time my father advised me to cut contact. He was right and deep down, I knew it.

"I don't care, family doesn't do that to their granddaughter. She is damn ignorant, that's all there is too it. You cannot fix that. Your mom has been trying all her life, Enola."

"I never want to see her again."

"You don't have too. We can talk to your mom about that. I'll be home soon; do you need me now?"

"No Dad. Love you."

"Ok ignore those people. Stay home. I'll see you soon."

I hung the phone back up on the charging base. I picked up my father's glass ash tray that sat near it. My father was a chain smoker, but often I could find cigarettes he only took a puff from, and then put out. I gathered them up and put them in an empty pack. I smoked outside by my house, and that is exactly where I was headed.

"Enola Wilson!" I heard my mother scream.

Oh shit, she said my full name. I am in trouble.

I put my cigarette out on the wooden bench I was sitting on. My parents had built it together years early.

"Yeah mom?" I yelled back.

She could hear me. She could smell the cigarette smoke; but she could not see me. There was a locked gate connected to our fenced in back yard. I opened it.

"Are you even kidding me, Enola?" Her tone changed.

"What?"

"You're smoking?" She asked.

"No. Why?" I played dumb.

"Why in the hell is that cigarette still smoking then, Enola?" She didn't fall for it.

"I don't know." I continued to play dumb.

"So, you didn't smoke it?"

"Nope." I was not going to budge.

"Did you tell Grandma 'Fuck you', Enola?" I already knew this is exactly why my mother was here.

"Yes, I did." I had already decided before her arrival, that I would bite the bullet and tell the truth.

"Why, Enola?" She asked.

"She said I was jealous of Amanda." I responded. "I told her 'Fuck you', twice."

"Enola you are grounded for speaking to an adult that way. I will deal with grandma." My mother said.

71

"I don't want to see her anymore." I added.

"Enola, I guess I can go without my mom and dad." She responded.

I did not know it then, but I know it now, she was using a guilt tactic on me. She was afraid to be alone, without her father. It had nothing to do with my grandmother.

"Not it's fine." I felt bad.

"Don't be on the internet. You are still grounded." She reminded me.

I was constantly grounded. My mother had once grounded me to my bedroom for six weeks straight. I was only permitted to come out to use the restroom. Not even for dinner. The internet being taken from me was a small punishment, I wasn't going to argue with my mother any further.

"I'm going to ask Grandma why she said that Enola."

"Ok." I responded.

My mother left. I went outside and crawled over to the bushes, closest my grandmother's house. I had hoped to be able to hear my mother. My mother did not knock as she normally would, rather, she barged in. After several minutes of not being able to see or hear anything, I went back inside. I laid back down my bed. I started to count the glow and the dark stars on my ceiling. I had just started to fall asleep when the telephone rang. The CALLER ID came across the television. It was someone from Grandma's.

"Hello."

"Enola if your mom ever puts her hands on Grandma again, I will have her put in jail. Do you understand me? You better tell her when she sobers up."

"Latrine?"

"Enola she will go to jail. You can't just assault people."

Latrine was talking to me like I had done it.

"Are you kidding me Latrine? Are you fucking kidding me? Fuck you and grandma." I snapped back.

"Enola, grandma's eyes are black." Latrine responded.

"Latrine, you are threatening to put my mother in jail over black eyes on an adult human, but you have sexually assaulted my entire childhood and she didn't put you in jail." I went on.

"Enola-"

"Don't Enola me. Maybe I will fucking put you in jail. How dare you. Maybe I will call children services myself again. This time, I won't lie for you guys I won't lie for any of you pieces of shit."

I hung the phone up. I screamed at the top of my lungs. Why was it always something? My mother had a way of making everything about her. Despite the things Latrine had done to me, and despite the fact my grandma closed her eyes to it all, I still didn't want her to be hurt. Physically or mentally. I was disgusted that my mother would do such a thing, but I was never going to turn against her... Or would I?

The drama was short lived. Latrine was suddenly back in prison. Amanda's parents did not approve of the relationship Latrine was having with their minor child, and unlike my mother, they were acting. Latrine was arrested on several sex crimes against a child. They had even consisted of a homemade pornography of Latrine and Amanda. Doug had got caught with it and told on Latrine for any and everything the detective could possibly be interested in. My mother had given me the details of both of their arrests. That was not the first time Doug had possession of a video like that, only the time I know of the girl was much, much younger.

Latrine and Doug were both sent away to prison. My grandmother and I still had not spoken since my outburst and my mother physically assaulting her. Amanda moved in with my grandmother when she turned eighteen. I still considered her a groomed victim. My grandparents had allowed her to stay in their home for years leading up to her turning eighteen. They had even hidden her as a runaway.

CHAPTER 15 GRADUATION

"Here you go, Enola." My grandmother was the first person to approach me after graduation. "Grandma is so proud of you."

I hugged grandma tightly. She had handed me something, and I knew it was jewelry, she had secretly transferred it from her hand to mine. I looked down into the palm of my hand and saw the prettiest piece of jewelry that I now own. My grandmother had a huge version of the necklace. She had purchased a smaller one of my mother, and now this one for me.

"I love this Grandma." I cried.

Grandma wasn't exactly the gift giving type. She always claimed she and Papal were poor, but I knew they weren't. Grandma came from poverty, so she was very possessive of what was hers and Papal's. It was theirs, not ours. She would help if she absolutely had to, but at minimum and then she rubbed it in your face for years. My mother is so similar.

"Take care of it, it's a good one. I got it from J.C. PENNEY." My grandma was proud.

"I will, I promise." I agreed.

My father grabbed my diploma out of my opposite hand.

"Let's make sure your name is on this and let's get out of here." My father joked.

My four years of high school were full of drama and heartache. I wasn't allowed to express my true needs without fear of repercussion, and nobody knew what actually happened to me, therefor I was widely misunderstood. I was left out of gatherings. I was left out of slumber parties and trips. I was judged as a child, while the adults in my life had failed me. My father only knew a mere portion of what I had been through. He trusted my mother would not lie to him about the things we had experienced or needed. My father was essentially a long-term victim of the sexual abuse I endured at Latrine's hands. We survived the toughest years of my life, together.

I saw the faces of so many familiar adults that day, who had turned their other cheek to the red flags I had displayed, in the gymnasium that day. I tried not to let it bother me. Some of my friends' parents had been extremely unkind. I had even been called a whore by one of them.

"You've got to be kidding, this says Kari- not Enola." My father had a look of panic on his face.

Kari quickly approached me, as our diplomas had accidentally been switched. My name was printed on a diploma. It was real. Enola Wilson graduated high school.

"Look, Dad." I handed the diploma to him.

"As much as we paid this school, you better have that." My mother added to the joke. She wanted to remind me that she paid for a portion of my education. She always rubbed it in my face and even used my attendance to the school as a form of torment. The summer before my senior year she had told me I was not allowed to attend. I reached out to a wealthier woman I knew within the school and voiced the concern my mother had shared with me about not being able to afford my last year of school. She told me one way or another, I would be there. I knew that meant even if she had to help fund it. My mother told her that I had made it all up, there was never any talk of me not attending the private school my senior year.

"Well, come on Enola. We had better get out of here before Coach sees you." My father further added to the comedy.

My freshman year, I had refused to take part in a project required to pass a class, that was required to graduate. I took the same class four times, with an "Incomplete" standing at the end of the year. Somehow the last quarter, it was marked complete. The teacher later told me he respected my will to stand against something I did not believe in, despite the adversity that I faced while doing it. I had really graduated. I could not believe it.

"I am so proud of you, Enola." Coach hugged me. "I will see you again. You will do great things, young lady."

"Thank you for everything you have done for me." I hugged coach tightly. Coach had been my security blanket all through high school. When others figured that out, my life had quickly changed, and for the better. "I love you, not as my teacher, but also as my friend."

The mediocre way that I thanked this man at graduation was insulting. He went well above and beyond the duties in his job description. He held my hand and talked me into wanting to live, somehow, during the darkest years of my life. 'Thanks' couldn't be all I had for him.

Maybe one day I will publish a best-selling novel, as Mrs. Duffner told me I would, and maybe I'll tell the world about Coach. I was blessed to experience his love and dignity firsthand. A teacher that absolutely loved his students. I will tell the world about him one day.

My father had an emotional encounter with Coach as we were leaving the building. My father was never angered that I turned to another human for the same advice he had already given me. He never envied my relationship with Coach, and he always thanked him for being so good to me. My mother hated him because he could see right through the situation. It wasn't too difficult to see once someone realized she was putting on a front. I headed out the door behind my mother to avoid the waterfall of tears I was nearing from Coach. I sat down on the front steps of the high school and took pictures with Mimi and Papal. Mimi always had hot flashes and she had gone outside to avoid being in the muggy gym any longer.

"You did it girl." Mimi put her arm around my shoulders. "I don't have to lie to that poor secretary anymore about your whereabouts."

"Thank God." I giggled.

"Good job, kiddo." Papal said.

Papal called me kiddo because he couldn't remember which kid I was. Although he spent most of his evenings at my single father's home ensuring he was properly parenting us, he forgot my brother and I first. He was very young, and full of life. Alzheimer's quickly took over his mind.

"I love you Papal." I hugged my grandfather.

His face was flushed. That happened when he didn't know exactly where he was, "I love you too." He winked at me.

"Let's go, I'm getting drunk." I told Mimi. It was no secret to my family that I had developed a drinking problem, despite my attempts to keep it from them. I was drinking to suppress my own reality, and everybody thought I was enjoying it. It was a subject I didn't speak on much.

"Jesus, you aren't even out of the church yet, Enola." Mimi was mad at me in an instant.

Mimi didn't drink and she didn't believe in anyone else drinking either. When she was a small child, her father had left a tavern and passed out at the wheel. He caused an accident that took the life of a teenage girl. Mimi never did get past that. I understand how she couldn't.

"I'm joking with ya." I said.

"Oh, but you're not." My father said.

"Encourage her to drink, that's cute." My mother added. She knew she was the one that had encouraged me to start drinking. She took me in my first bar at fourteen, and taught me to drink beer from bottles, she said the keg would get me drunker, faster, that I should avoid it. She just wanted to say something rude. By now, I knew she talked, just to be talking.

My father was having my graduation party at his house, immediately following graduation. My parents could not agree to have one party because my mother insisted on inviting Latrine and his now family. My father's family couldn't bear to be around Latrine. Mimi had prepared the party before graduation and her girlfriends were at Dad's finishing up anything Mimi didn't get done. My father had me an amazing party. My mother did not attend it.

I stepped out front and called my mother when I had first arrived home. It was a habit all my life that prior to enjoying myself, I had to make sure my mother was not mad at me. I asked her so much, that everyone that knew us would joke and ask me if I were mad at them, when they saw me anywhere.

"Are you mad at me Mom?" She answered the third time I called her.

"No, Enola, other than the ugly dress and flats you picked out."
She responded. My mother had promised to take me shopping for a dress
and shoes for graduation for weeks leading up to my special day. Every day
she had a new excuse as to why she could not go, and everyday turned into
tomorrow. Tomorrow never did come for our shopping trip. Mimi had
taken me at the last minute. She had made a comment about what I was
wearing before my graduation ceremony even began.

"I'm sorry." She knew how to instantly make me cry. She did it
often.

"Oh, I didn't mean to make you cry, Enola." My mother said.

"I'm almost six foot tall. I can't wear heals." I defended my choice
of shoes. I constantly entered fight mode when it came to my mother.
Fright was eliminated from the equation by this point, and I was too
stubborn too flight.

"Quit your damn whining." She insisted.

"You should've got me shoes if you wanted me to wear certain
shoes. But you didn't." My heart felt like it hit my stomach. I didn't often
fire back at my mother.

"Cry me a river, Enola. Shit happens. The world doesn't revolve
around—"

"Your world has never revolved around me." I interrupted her and
hung up on her.

I entered the house. My father and I locked eyes. He had
recommended that I didn't call her often. I thought he was attempting to
alienate her from my life, but now I know he knew it was for the better. She
had no love to offer me, not even the day I graduated high school.

"She said something mean to you?" My father asked.

"Yeah, about my shoes." I responded.

"She has quite some nerve, don't she?"

My father had heard me complain every day for two months about my
shoes and dress. He had offered to take me, but it had been important for
me to reserve this for her. All my friends and their mothers had gone.

"Yes." I responded, "I'm going to change."

I went into my bedroom and grabbed my darkening curtain to close off
the window. I let go of the curtain and pulled the other open, I could not
believe what I was seeing. The family of squirrels were on the electric wire
outside of my house. There were five of them.

Uncle squirrel, is that you? Please do not hurt baby squirrel. Baby squirrel, RUN!

Suddenly, they all took off. I shut the curtains and changed into my short and t-shirt. I knew the night ahead of me would be a wild one. I was not joking with Mimi, I was serious. I was getting drunk, and then leaving for vacation a small group of friends, where I would remain drunk. I had only planned to remain drunk for a week, it might have lasted years.

I turned on my vanity light. I still, clenched in the palm of my hand, held onto the diamond charm my grandmother had handed me an hour earlier. I put it on and admired it. I could not imagine the thought of something happening to it, so I took it back off, and hid it. I had a premonition of an enemy ripping it off in a bar. My grandmother had never given me such a gift, and it was valuable to me. I freshened up my horrifically done make up, and headed out to the back yard, where my father and the people that truly loved me, were gathered to celebrate my success.

I looked around. It was always the same group of good people my father had surrounded me with during my time with him. I didn't realize it then, but I do now, that's all I needed. Again, the expectation that I had set for my mother was only a figment of my imagination. I can't explain the desire I had to be a part of her family, even though they brought me down. It would take years to process this trauma.

CHAPTER 16 HEAVEN CRIED

I do not think I had ever prayed as intensely as I did the day Papal passed away. I sat near his hospital bed, and gently caressed his harm. This angered my grandmother as she insisted it was causing him pain. I suspected per usual, she was jealous of the love we were showing Papal and not her, even though he was dying. We all knew he was already gone, and she remained in denial. She was angry with Papal; not upset the way one would expect a man of that many years wife to act. She had time and time again expressed that she could not believe he was leaving her to deal with this mess alone. She was angry at him for being sick, and even angrier at him for dying. He left her alone, far too soon.

Her kids were a mess. Three out of four of them are addicts. Two out of four are pedophiles. The grandchildren were mostly all following the lead of their parents.

Papal was not sick the month before, undiagnosed lung cancer had suddenly begun to kill him. I was scared, scared of what was to come in the days ahead without Papal. I knew exactly what his death would do to my mother.

On November 8, 2009, my grandfather took his last breath. I looked up at my mother when they pronounced Papal dead. It looked as if her soul had left her body, as if she had died with him for a moment in time. Not a single emotion lived within her. My mother's heart was broken. Papal was the only living human that understood my mother, and I believe he was the only unconditional love she ever knew. When Papal died, a part of my mother certainly did too. She has never replaced the spark she lost that day. We all have our own person and Papal was my mother's, and without him, she was suddenly lost.

I watched Papal take his last breath two weeks after being admitted to the hospital. He was gone, dead, just like that, and he wasn't coming back. I was surrounded by my mother's family the moment Papal passed away. I remember actually thinking to myself, that now this room contained my grandfather's dead body and a whole lot of deep dark family secrets. My mother's pain had consumed me, I could always feel her pain. Latrine standing right beside me, was a part of those secrets, a huge part of them.

My grandfather kept them quiet, tightly concealed within the realm of the family. He had convinced my mother to 'fix it', per say. He knew just how to keep the peace between everyone, something my grandmother knew she would not succeed at. We did not respect her.

The day of the funeral quickly arrived. It was there that I realized some crucial things for the very first time.

My grandmother was traumatized by Papal's death. She had never dealt with a single issue on her own, he always picked her up out of the battlefield, and provided a shield of defense for her. None of us were allowed to disagree with her, and if we did Papal was upset with us. It was always her way, or no way because she would disappear for days on end if she did not get her away. Sometimes she took a few bottles of liquor in her small travel bag and did that anyways. That day, she wanted to get home to her comfortable place. Papal was gone and she was drained. I could see it in her eyes. She was broken. She did not have any idea how she was going to continue living her life without him.

"Pick a pot of flowers Enola." Grandma said to me as she pointed out the flowers lining the church wall that were not yet spoken for.

"I'll take this one." I picked a beautiful pot of flowers up that had been placed off to the side by itself.

My grandmother abruptly yanked the pot of flowers out of my hand, "No you will not take this one Enola, it is sitting off to the side because my sister and her child molesting husband, JJ sent it, and we will not be accepting it."

We all knew my aunt Bozo had been brutally raped for many years during her childhood, by her uncle, but it was a forbidden topic, and we knew we were not to speak on it, but I had a question, that could not wait. I didn't care what the circumstances were.

"Then why is it ok for him to be sitting here with me?" I asked as Latrine sat right beside me, after brutally raping me for many years. I had always wondered why my relationship with Latrine wasn't treated as Bozo's with JJ: Nonexistent.

"Enola, not here, for once this isn't about you." My grandmother quickly fired her words back at me. This was a common come back she used, and not just with me but her words always felt like bullets into my heart.

"You won't see me again after this is all over, will you Enola?" Latrine selfishly asked.

He knew Papal was the glue that held the family together. He also knew by now I wasn't wearing a filter. I was going to say, whatever it was I had to say. I compared him to the "silent rapist of the family". He was him, in a new form. I see him no different than my grandmother seen JJ.

We buried Papal that November, but the secrets did not get buried with him. In fact, they blossomed, bigger than ever before, as if he watered them himself.

Christmas was there shortly after Papal's death, and the family was back together again. They were all still clearly mourning the loss of Papal. I was not though. I was mad. I suddenly realized I was sitting there with a group of people that did not think I was human enough to be protected from my childhood rapist, as he his wife and his three babies were present in the same room that I was. I didn't deserve to ever have to look at Latrine again.

My mother had groomed me all these years to believe this behavior was acceptable, to believe you should forgive a person for such heinous acts they committed against you as a small child. I had disclosed the details of my sexual abuse to my mother, seven years before that Christmas. Latrine was welcome in her home, at my birthday parties and I was still made to stay with my grandmother.

It was the first holiday my husband had spent with my family. We were sitting in the basement on the couch, right outside the dungeon. Latrine no longer occupied the dungeon, but it still gave me a leery feeling. One glimpse into it and my entire childhood filled with abuse flashed back to me in an instance. Nobody seemed to ever care, or even consider that this may bother me. I watched Latrine's daughters play and giggle together. I had just had a miscarriage, the sight of a baby already made me cry, but his babies? Why could he have babies and I could not? It was not fair. I do not know what took place in my mind that day, but I had a complete mental reset as far as that part of my family went. My grandparents had fully funded a fertility to fix Latrine, so that him and Amanda could start a family. They were married shortly after his release from prison. She was barely legal.

"Come on babe, let's go home, I just can't do this." I leaned in towards my husband's ear and quietly, but passionately spoke those words that were seemed life changing for me. I had finally made my own decision. I was making the decision to end the mental exhaustion I had been enduring all the years I was forced to see Latrine. It was the first time I would abruptly exit the family gathering, and it was the last one I would ever attend. I suddenly loathed my dead grandfather. Not one ounce of me mourned him ever again after that day.

"I'm sorry, I know it's hard without your grandpa." My husband spoke softly back to me as he rubbed the back of my tensed-up neck.

"It's not because of that." I became defensive toward my sweet husband that had never hurt me. "Come on, I'll tell you in the car." I grabbed my knock off Chanel bag and we proceeded out the front door. I took a breath. I could not believe I had made it out without a single person confronting me.

"Where are you going Enola?" My grandmother confronted me at the doorway. I looked back and down at the stairs, each stair was lined with a child and a plate of food, all the cousins were enjoying each other.

"Home, Grandma." I spoke loud and clear, so that everyone could hear me. I was trying hard not to cry.

"Drama Queen, just like your mama" I could smell the alcohol on my grandmother's breath as usual, "Don't you think if anyone misses Big Latrine, it's me?" She always displayed such a high level of jealousy when it came to Papal, no matter who she was speaking to. When she called him by name, she was in that kind of drunk mood, the type a young woman would be fearful of, and I was. I was fearful as to what she was about to say in front of my husband. I had still accepted responsibility for everything I had been through. I carried the weight of the fault for many years.

"It's not about Papal." I talked back to her, and Papal was not there to stop me anymore.

My mother had remained silent through the beginning of the conversation that was quickly escalating with hostility. "Mom she's because you're child molesting son in here, and that's her choice." My mother defended me. The last time my mother defended me, my grandmother kicked us out of the house and belittled me as a small girl. The topic of Latrine raping me, was a topic that was avoided.

I sat down into the ground and pulled fur lined boots onto my feet; I was stepping on the heels of them. I was trying to avoid the still escalating conversation that was taking place one flight of stairs below me.

The last thing I heard was, "They were two kids playing". My aunt that held an eighth-grade education had just summed up my childhood with three disgusting words, "two kids playing." That will forever ring in my ears. It was not the first time I heard it, and it certainly was not the last time that I heard it.

I ran to the car quickly and opened the door. I slammed it shut and quickly locked the doors once my husband got in.

"What don't I know, Enola?" he was confused by all the brand-new information he just heard.

I had felt such shame and embarrassment at the thought of revealing the years of sexual abuse I had endured at the hands of Latrine. I still felt like I should have told sooner, and because I did not, I was just as much at fault. I was petrified of what my husband and his family would think of me if they knew the details of the abuse, that made up so much of my life.

"Latrine raped me, molested me, and did so many other horrible things to me when I was a little girl." I broke down again. I bawled, hysterically. My mother always used the term, "molest" but I knew how much worse the correct term made my situation. Rape. It was a term my family was fearful of using, it would have meant acknowledging they knew it was wrong, and it was not ever two kids playing. My uncle raped me, so many times, and I finally told someone other than my mother or her family. My husband held me so tight that night. We sat in the driveway of our small two bedroom mobile that night for hours. Mimi had purchased me the mobile home so that I could live on my own, the summer that I graduated.

"You deserve so much better than this, I don't care what she says." My husband said, as he moved by bangs out of my face.

"I know." I did know too. I knew I had been dealt an unfortunate hand in some areas of my life. I just did not know then I did not have to deal with it forever. I vowed to stay away from Latrine forever that night, even if it meant staying away from all of them. I had to be strong, for me now. The uphill battle had just begun, again.

CHAPTER 17 LIZZY

"Get her out of here." I looked at the nurse and I meant what I said.

My local hospital was jokingly nicknamed "Dead Central". I had just unexpectedly delivered a one-pound baby. I don't remember walking into the hospital, but I remember waking up. My husband was standing beside me and there was an alien look alike human, that was mine... in an incubator right in front of me. Our lives had drastically changed in an instant.

"Baby it's ok. She is from the life flight team. Is her name still Lizzy?" My husband spoke softly, but clearly to me. I was highly medicated, and he wanted me to understand exactly what I was signing and saying.

"Yes, Lizzy." I responded. Papal had died two years prior. Latrine's second daughter was born shortly before he passed away. He begged Latrine to call her Izzy. He loved the name. Latrine did not name his child Lizzy. I knew I was pregnant while standing at my grandfather's death bed. I knew before anyone told me that she was a girl, and that I would call her Lizzy. "Lizzy Lynn." I followed up.

My mother's middle name is Lynn.

"Are you sure, Enola?" My husband asked.

"Yes." I answered with confidence.

The life flight nurse took down the information that I had just given her. "There's a storm coming, we have to get this baby to Children's." She expressed the need to move quickly.

"Thank you." I knew Lizzy needed to be in a bigger, better hospital. She was not even considered viable, but they saved her anyways. I offered gratitude to the team as they exited the room, even though I was not entirely sure of what was going on.

I looked around the room. My family had filled the entire room up. I felt some type of way about my Grandma Jean being there and I knew it right away. I looked at her after I had looked at Lizzy and immediately remembered the things, she allowed to happen to me. We had long moved past the damage she had done to me as a child, or had we? Nevertheless, I had instant feeling of fear when I saw Grandma near Lizzy. I knew I must be crazy to be having such vile thoughts about this now, little old lady.

Lizzy was gone, rushed down the hallway and into the elevator, where she would be pushed onto the roof of this hospital, and boarding a flight, all before she's even one hour old.

"You can't even have a baby without drama?" My mother joked in front of everyone. Everyone seemed to find the comedy in my mother's words. I didn't. They would forever stick with me. I didn't speak much to my family. I was exhausted and quite honestly, wanted everyone to leave.

"Dad, I just had surgery, Lizzy could die, please make everyone but hubby, you and mom leave." I whispered to my father, in tears.

He kindly shuffled my family and friends out of the room. I felt helpless and humiliated, and I had to plan my escape so that I could be with Lizzy.

"Enola, calm down honey." My father rubbed my head. "You have been through a lot today." He reiterated that several times. I had learned to handle a lot, and never leave time for myself to heal over the years.

"Where's the doctor, cause I'm leaving." I was not asking, I was telling.

"You just had an unplanned emergency surgery, Enola." My husband said.

"I'm out of here, I'm going with the baby, you coming?" My mother was looking at my father.

"Lizzy is going to the best hospital, perhaps in the state of Ohio. My daughter's blood pressure was just so high they called her episode a mini stroke, and she's just had her infant she couldn't even touch taken from her." My father seemed upset my mother had asked him to go. "I am staying with Enola." My father had just told my mother how he felt and didn't care. I heard the tone in his voice, he was upset with her. I later found out she had just made a joke to my father about me wanting him in the delivery room, even though she was there. He knew a normal mother would be offended, and she made jokes about it. These types of things bothered my father much more than they did me. If he was there with me, I didn't care that she wasn't. Same old routine, a different situation.

"Ok. Enola. I will call you. Can I go on the life flight with her?" My mother asked.

"Yes, please do." I needed her to stare at Lizzy the entire way there. I gave her strict instructions not to remove her eyes of my brand-new baby girl.

"Ok, I won't let you down." My mother took off down the hallway.

I laid back and looked around the room. I have never been an optimistic person, and all I could think is that my precious girl wasn't going to make it. She was so fragile, and so tiny. I had never even imagined a human could be the small and breathe. I could see through Lizzy's skin. I could see her veins. Her toes were still webbed. I couldn't believe it. My tiny human was going to have to fight to survive.

Why is this happening to me? Please God, let her live. Take me and not Lizzy. Please let her live.

"Get the doctor." I demanded my husband.

"He will be in soon, Enola, I swear you are the worlds worse hospital patient, Enola. I already warned him." My father was annoyed.

My husband got up and left the room anyways. He came back with a doctor.

"I'm ready to leave." I exclaimed.

"Not quite yet, you aren't." The doctor was monotone. He had not offered me false hope. In fact, he had told me the worse possible scenarios so I knew exactly what could happen, positively and negatively. "What's your pain level and be honest, I need to know what to send you off with, when are discharged."

"Seven." I responded. I was so tired; I could hardly stand myself.

"Ok. We will meet tomorrow morning." He said.

I could tell that I was leaving in the morning. If my precious baby girl survived the night, I would be at her side tomorrow. I was leaving, either way. I laid down on my side. My father left shortly after the doctor visited for the last time. I think he knew how tired I was. Suddenly it dawned on me that Mimi was on vacation. She was twelve hundred miles away from me.

"Babe, did you tell Mimi? I asked.

"Your dad did." He said, "She was taking the next flight home, Enola."

"Ok. I'm so seepy." I always left the l out of the word sleepy when I was severely tired, intentionally. It is one of my many childlike habits.

"I love you, Enola and I'm so proud of you." My husband hugged me.

"I love you too." I closed my eyes.

I fell asleep for two hours that night, and when I woke back up, I was up for the day. I was leaving that hospital soon to be with Lizzy. Seven A.M. came soon.

"How are you today?" The Doctor asked.

"I'm fine, and I'm ready to leave... Even if you say I can't, I am leaving anyways. I need to see my baby." I made sure he knew my mind had not changed.

"You just had a C-section, yesterday. You will need to be transported in a wheelchair." The doctor took a deep breath. "I normally would never discharge a cesarean patient, but under the circumstances, I'd like for you to be able to see your newborn."

"Thank you." I responded.

After checking all my vitals from the night before, the doctor typed a few things into the computer.

ENOLA

"The nurse will be in shortly." He said as he left the room. "Good luck to you."

Let's go. My husband had already packed all my stuff back up. The hospital was loaning us a wheelchair given the circumstances. He lifted me into a standing position. He knew my abdominal pain was too severe to lift myself up. I was comfortably in the wheelchair, waiting for the nurse.

"Monya!!" I couldn't believe my eyes. "Is this real?" I had encountered Monya several months prior. She was the registered nurse that I was assigned after a very emotional miscarriage. Monya gently cared for me that day. If you were to ask me now, the top five people who have left an impression on me, Monya would be one of them. She seen the little girl hurting inside of me, and maybe the lack of love I was receiving.

"Honey, I gave you pictures of your beautiful little Lizzy, yesterday." She explained.

"I didn't notice that it was you through all the chaos and masks, Monya. Thank you."

Monya wasn't just a nurse. She wasn't just there do to her job and leave at the end of the day. I can probably speak for all her patients, when I say Monya left her mark on me. Monya had photographed my brand-new baby girl the second she was born. I was under anesthesia and did not get to see her. "I wasn't sure if you would wake up before they took her." Monya said.

"I did, and I saw her, she was beautiful, Monya." I reached out for Monya to hug me.

"Awe, you be careful, Enola." Monya hugged me tightly.

"I will, thank you for everything you have done for me." I wanted Monya to know I appreciated her. She made me feel safe and loved. She believed in me and had only met me twice.

"Take care of my girl!" Monya joked with my husband.

My husband wheeled me out of Dead Central the next day. I recall a long hallway, over a rode way, with many windows once we reached the next hospital where Lizzy was. It took you from the parking garage to the hospital. My husband gently pushed me to the hospital. The hallway felt like it was miles long. We went down a glass elevator that took us to the NICU. My husband stopped me at the doors, he once again tried to prepare me for how little Lizzy was. I had seen her, but I was on all kind of medication and anesthetic still.

Nothing could have prepared me for the tiny human I was about to see. My daughter. Her fingers and toes were still webbed. I could see each one of her rib bones through her skin. Her eyes had not yet opened, and she had tiny blond curls. She was so tiny, and so precious.

The moment I laid eyes on my sweet little baby girl, I knew things in my life were going to change, and forever. I would never again attend a family event with anyone related to my mother. I would protect my sweet little girl at all costs. I would never hurt her, the way they had hurt me. I knew it the second I saw her. Lizzy changed my life, forever.

The following year I birthed another beautiful premature baby. He was much bigger than Lizzy and did not have any medical issues. Jayden, the baby that would complete our family. I had everything I ever wanted. My beautiful blond-haired, blue-eyed babies, and my husband. The happy family I always wanted my own mother to be a part of. I was finally living it, my dream. Things were not always perfect, but we were always together as one.

CHAPTER 18 DISCLOSE THE DETAILS

I had long awaited my appointment with the urology specialist. I had to travel over an hour, after I waited four and a half months to be seen, as I was on state insurance, and access to a specialist is often limited. I anxiously awaited my turn to see the doctor.

"Enola Wilson," the nurse called my name.

I followed her down a hallway where she collected my weight and took me into a room for my vitals.

"Doctor Chaco has a resident with him today, will that be an issue for you?"

I panicked. Yes, this was a huge issue for me. It had taken every day of the four and a half months to prepare myself to be seen by a male physician. I had always seen females. "No." I lied.

"Ok, I'm going to leave your gown, they will be in shortly, everything off from the waist down."

"Ok." I timidly responded.

She exited the room. I took my clothing off from the waist down and draped myself with the small blue disposable cloth they provided me with. I was panicking. A knock at the door.

"Mrs. Wilson?" It was the doctor, "may we enter?"

"Yes."

They entered the room. A duo of male doctors. The main doctor explained to me the reason and the purpose of the resident doctor being present. I understood, he needed to learn, and a learning experience is just what he received, me too.

"Chronic UTI's?" He asked.

"Yes, and constant symptoms." I responded.

"How long has this been going on?"

"Since I was really young." I answered him honestly. "Five or six."

He sat down on the stool at the end of the chair. "Scoot all the way down, until you can't anymore." The awkward phrase you always hear when visiting the lady doctor.

I scooted. He put his gloves on.

"I'm going to apply a small bit of pressure, just to take a look."

I tensed up but didn't speak a word. There were two men, I had never seen before, fully investigating my vagina.

"Scar tissue." The resident doctor said.

"Yes, a mass amount. It's old scar tissue." The doctor replied. He removed his speculum from inside of me. "Personal question..."

"Yes?" I could not imagine what he was going to ask me. I was so uneasy to begin with.

"Were you sexually abused?"

"Yes." I felt the tears filling up. My chest got heavy; an anxiety attack was stewing. "Can I just speak to you?" I asked the doctor.

"Yes, I want you both to understand, when a patient has been a victim of sexual abuse, it is especially important that you communicate that with your health care provider, so we don't end up in situations where the patient is experiencing flash backs. Your mental health is so important to us." The doctor explained.

"Yes, it is." The other agreed.

I covered up, and he exited the room.

"You do have slight internal damage, which is almost always a result of being abused as a child."

I had no idea a medical professional would accommodate me because of what I had been through. I had endured many uncomfortable OBGYN visits that this information could have benefited me in knowing.

The doctor explained to me what he thought was going on with my health, and the details of how it would be treated.

I left there feeling respected that day and I left with answers. I had been sick frequently all my life with these infections. I would finally seek some sort of relief.

CHAPTER 19 HISTORY REPEATS ITSELF

Responding to my mother's long term boyfriends' cries for help had become a regular occurrence the summer Bubba left for the service. Steven had been around for most of our lives. We met him before our dad even moved out, eighteen years prior. Steven never married my mother and still to this day lives out of a suitcase and goes home to his own mothers to shower. The summer Bubba left, Steven spent more time at my mother's, he knew her mental state was not well, and he worried what the alcohol added to it would do to her. So was I.

"Enola, she is suicidal." He barely let me say Hello.

"I'll be over." I hung the phone up. I looked in the back seat at Lizzie and Jayden and gave second thought into taking them with me. I wasn't sure if time was on my side. You never know what my mother will really do. I proceeded toward my mother's home. Little did I know this day would be the beginning to the end of my relationship with her. We arrived at my mother's home. Steven was in the driveway with no shirt on. His chest was bright red. I did not have to ask what happened to him; I knew it was from my mother punching him. I knew without asking. My mother was full of anger and rage, and just as she did when I was a small girl, she was still drinking and letting it all out, in the wrong ways.

I didn't speak to Steven when I saw him. I know my mother and presumed she was looking out the window. If she were mad at Steven, it would fuel her flame if I spoke to him. I had learned how to deal with my mother. I knocked on her door. Before I could even speak a word, my mother lunged onto the front porch, and closed fist hit me in the side of the head. I grabbed the side of my head. I was in shock. I looked back at my car and saw that Lizzy seen what her grandmother had just done to me. I looked back at my mother. She had drawn her arm back to hit me again. She had that blank, empty look in her eyes. The one that used to terrify me so much. She noticed me nearing the back side of her concrete porch. She grabbed my hair and threw me off the porch. I looked up again and Lizzy had her hand on the car window, and a big tear streaming down her face. I could not believe my mother had just abused me, a now grown woman, in front of my child.

"Don't come here again, Enola. I hate you." My mother slurred her words.

"I was only coming to visit, Mom." My mother had put me on the ground, and I remained there in a still position. She had really hurt my feelings more than she physically hurt me. All I could think about is the time I heard Grandma kick us out of the family. My children heard every word just she spoke.

"Fuck you, Enola." My mother went back inside. She began to bang her head on the glass windows.

I was fearful she would break one and cut her head up. I could not negotiate with my mother that day. The next thing I knew the garage door was opening, and her reverse lights were on in her little yellow beat-up car. My car was parked behind her. I knew it a drunken rage she would without a doubt back into it, even with her grandchildren present inside. I moved my car. I got out and called the sheriff's department. I spoke loudly so that my mother could hear me. I read her plate number off, just in case she left. She quickly shut the garage door and within moments the entire house was black.

The sheriff pulled in.

"My mother is mentally ill. She had legitimate mini strokes, and heart issues. I want you to know this before you approach her." I explained.

"I know exactly who she is, the drunk of the Duchess Bar." The officer joked.

Did he really just?

"Do you live here?" He asked.

"No." I responded.

"Did you ever?" He followed up.

"Not really." I responded again, "he does, kinda." I pointed at Steven.

"Can you let me in?" He asked Steven.

Steven unlocked the doors and entered in front of the sheriff. He called out for my mother, but she didn't answer. The officer asked where my mother was. Steven told the officer she must be in her bedroom. Before anyone else could speak, the officer kicked my mother's bedroom door off the hinges and tackled her to the floor. Nothing in this world, has ever upset me more, than seeing my small mother, tackled by a man triple her size. He never even tried to talk her out of the room, even after I told him she had mental problems.

"Enola, help me."

My mother looked pitiful. She had drank most of the days of the summer, and she had never been right. I couldn't help her. Nobody could. She needed admitted to a psychiatric unit, not jail. The same woman that just assaulted me in front of her grandchildren, needed my help.

"Listen to him, Mom. I'll come and get you when you sober up." I put my head down.

"She is going to jail until Monday, at the least."

He dragged my mother rather violently back out to the police cruiser. She would not look at me. Both of my children saw their grandmother get arrested that day. As I drove home, I realized my mother was letting history repeat itself. I had seen my own grandmother get arrested several times. I knew that was the last time I would take my children around my mother. I just did not know when I would be strong enough to tell her that I was intentionally keeping them away from her.

The next few days went by and no talk of the situation with my mother was mentioned, except by Bubba, who told me to stop beating myself up, reassuring me he would have done the same thing. We were out to dinner as a family, Bubba included, when my phone rang. My mother had gotten out of jail and Steven had told her all the things she had done to me. My mother was sobbing on the other end of the line, apologizing to me. She promised she would never touch alcohol again. A promise I already knew was broken because I had heard it so many times before. My mother needed help, and I had already realized the only way for me to hold her accountable, would be to cut her completely off, and that was a process, this was the beginning.

I had refused to press charges against my mother for assault when asked. I refused to speak about the things she did to me that day to the officer. She was still my mother, and that charge would have ended her career, forever. I am not sure why I cared so much about her career or wellbeing, she never cared about mine. I had asked myself for the first time that day, 'why am I still speaking to her?''.

CHAPTER 20 I AM ENOLA WILSON

"My name is Enola Wilson. A few years ago, my husband and I were in a bind, with three young children. My father selflessly moved out of his home so that we could have a stable home with our children, rather than risking another rental property we were occupying be sold. My grandmother still lived two houses down the street. She and I sat down together prior to me moving my family into my childhood home. She agreed that Latrine would keep his distance, and not travel past my home, as he had done when I still lived with my father. Latrine, my uncle, had taunted me for many years after raping me, physically abusing me, and molesting me as a small girl." I took a deep breath.

"Mrs. Wilson, may I ask, how old you were when he sexually assaulted you."

"Uh... Yes, your honor." I took a deep breath. I was on the line of losing it. "I was five years old the first time, and eleven years old the last time. He stopped when he went to prison for another sex crime." I was leaving nothing out.

"So, your uncle was a child too, or he was not?" She asked.

"Your honor, he was fifteen years old the first time he raped me. He was an adult the last time, though." I did not want Latrine to have any leniency. He was fully aware of what he was doing, and he knew that it was wrong. If he hadn't, he wouldn't have told me not to tell.

"Continue you on, Mrs. Wilson." The magistrate documented my answers and gave me back her full attention.

"He stayed away for a few years, but recently he has been harassing me. A few months ago, my grandmother was extremely intoxicated, she invited my children in her house. Latrine was inside. I have advised my grandmother and Latrine that he would never be anywhere near my children. I did attempt to reconcile with my grandmother, though. I believe she was luring my children that day. I have no choice but to believe that. She knew what Latrine was, and she knew my daughter was a replica of me, at the same age Latrine had assaulted me. My grandmother, I believe, was acting with a purpose. Anyways, recently he has drove past my house regularly, I make my kids come inside every time. It has been every day lately. I no longer feel safe in my own home. He and his wife Amanda, taunt me. He will yell profanities out the window, and she will give me an evil stare, until I can no longer see her. She has even thrown her arms up, signifying a fight to me. Anyways, most recently, last night, I was on my couch. My surveillance camera went off. I pulled the camera up and saw my little girl running full speed down the sidewalk. I have this footage with me here today, Your Honor, she gets to the door and expresses to her brother, 'He scares me to death.'. Right before she tells my son that Latrine speeds by on his motorcycle, rather than turning into my grandmother's driveway. He saw the fear in her, and followed her, just because he can. Your Honor, a mix of things happened here. Seeing my little girl run down the same sidewalk from the same man that raped me as a child, disturbed my mental state, and it wasn't necessary. I deserve peace. My uncle Latrine is still abusing me. I go outside after this all went down, and he is screaming, 'It's a free country, watch yourself, Bitch." He kept saying the same thing over again. I became extremely agitated. This was all after I had sent a letter to his house, asking him to please avoid going past mine. Your Honor, I can't take it anymore. I cannot live another single day like this. I have done my part. I cut them all out of my life, even my mother. I deserve to feel at home and safe in my own home. This has gone on for far too long. Latrine once told me if I spoke about this abuse I had endured, he would not only end my brother's life, but mine too." I started crying.

"He said what, Mrs. Wilson. Could you repeat that last sentence?"

"Yes, Your Honor, he told me he would kill me if I ever told anyone. I have told nearly one hundred thousand people on my viral social media platform. I am scared for my life, Your Honor." I sighed.

"I can and will keep him from your home. I am granting you this emergency order of protection. He will have the opportunity to provide evidence that he has not done any of the things listed in this complaint. He may bring witness, and even a lawyer. Sometimes, these lawyers are harsh." She flipped the page. "Also, I have put special instructions in this order, if Latrine must visit his mother, he will not be allowed outside of the home, or access to travel past your home."

"Thank you." I did not care about anything beyond the word granted. For the first time, in my life, I would be able to go months without seeing Latrine, hopefully forever without seeing Latrine. When you take the innocence of a little girl, I guess you sometimes lose your rights to take whatever route you want. Now Latrine will know what it is like to be stuck in a place and told that you can't come out. A place that was once your home. When you intentionally disturb a person mentally and out of your way, it turns into stalking. Stalking is illegal. Finally, he had to stay away from me.

I left the courthouse that day feeling free. Although I was only there for an order of protection, to keep Latrine away from my home, it was the first time the secret had left the realm of the family.

'ENOLA WILSON VS LATRINE WILSON'

I had waited decades to see this on paper. It was the first time I would hold Latrine accountable in court, but it would not be the last. I hope he knew his legal battle had just started.

CHAPTER 21 NOT ALONE

The day had arrived. I did not wake up that morning, because I never went to sleep the night before. An entire month and a half had gone by since I had seen Latrine. I felt like a new woman walking into the courtroom, surely not the damsel in distress that I was the first time I came in, alone with no attorney, to seek relief on my own behalf.

As soon as my husband and I arrived at the courthouse, I stepped out of the car and see Latrine and Amanda. Latrine kept driving as if he didn't notice me, but Amanda stared deep into my eyes. The last time she had been in this courthouse, she was the victim, standing in my place, forced by her parents. He had groomed her for many years, but I could no longer look at her as a victim. It has been twenty plus years now; she has made the decision to stay with him. I assume it is some psychological traumatic tie she has to him, but that didn't change the fact she allowed him access to two little girls, behind closed doors for the world to forget about, perhaps like they did me? Those girls are teenagers now, I think of them each time I see Latrine. I can only pray he was too afraid to touch them, because people like him do not change.

I walked into my attorney's office that morning, with a stack full of counseling records. These records consisted of years' worth private and cognitive group therapy settings. The same conclusion was typed out on each visit summary: sexually assaulted by uncle. My story never changed. I just was not allowed to give all the details. I was told by my mother years prior that I may end up in a home that wasn't that of a family member if this situation escalated. I knew my limits. The file still contained enough incriminating evidence against Latrine.

"Oh, what have we here?" Jon opened the folder and read the first page, that confirmed my dates as a patient at the psychiatric facility. "This is a game changer, Enola. Your uncle already agreed to sign this and stay away from you, but he was adamant about it only being effective for a year. I'm going to get you the full amount with this."

"He what?" I interrupted Jon before he was done speaking, "he didn't say I made it all up?" I was shocked.

"No, he didn't." Jon seemed shocked too.

"I just want him to stay away. Do you have the video?" I asked.

"Yep." Jon concluded. "I'll see you over there. You're ok, this is about him not you. A judge shouldn't have to tell a man that raped a child to stay away from her as an adult, that's common sense."

My husband and I walked out of Jon's office. His small practice is next door to the courthouse. We entered and took the stairs to the third floor. I opened the door to the mediation office, where our hearing would take place in the courtroom behind it.

"Enola Wilson." I quietly spoke my name to the court receptionist.

"Mrs. Wilson, you have an entire room waiting for you." She grinned.

"I do?" I asked.

We followed her to the conference room she had filled with my supporters. She opened the door. I was shocked. My cousins were there, my aunts and uncle were there, my father was there and most importantly, my eighty-one-year-old Mimi was there. Mimi intimidated my mother's family. I think Mimi is everything my grandmother wanted to be. Mimi is pure but her love for me is fierce, and now that she is old and doesn't hear well, she gets away with saying just about anything, to anyone. She uses it to her advantage, even though she would say I'm full of it.

"Hi." I smiled. I had only recently told my father and his family the details of the extent of my abuse as a child. My mother is a narcissist and had a way of hiding things. There's a reason she was not present in that conference room to support me, because she knew she had hidden so much. I held her accountable, and she ran. Literally, she bought a camper and moved twelve hundred miles away to work during the global pandemic. My grandmother once ran away to Tennessee to avoid a court date, they had so much in common.

"I love you guys, thank you." I expressed how grateful I was to my family. They already knew it, though. I loved these people. They had been there for every important moment of my life, and now my kids' lives. My own uncle, my father's brother, has never missed a single event I have had for one of my kids. This is a rare group of people, that I will forever hold onto and cherish. They say it takes a village, but my small circle seems just as dependable.

"Enola?" Jon opened the door.

"Yeah."

"I need, just you."

I stepped outside of the conference room. The hallway was quiet. Jon was not though. "He has requested not to be present in the court room with you." He giggled.

"I wouldn't expect anything more of Latrine." I responded. I'm not sure why but him asking not to be around me, after he had driven past my home for twenty years and taunted me, after he had raped my precious little body. He sure had some audacity. I had mentally prepared myself to face him.

"Yeah, but he's signing this and agreeing to everything you asked for."

"Oh, god bless him, a few hundred dollars and two decades later, he's going to stay away from me?"

"Let's go, just answer her honestly, and I'll do most of the talking."

We walked into the courtroom. It was empty other than Jon, me, the magistrate and Latrine's attorney.

"Mrs. Wilson, has attorney Felts explained to you that Latrine Wilson will be signing a consent agreement here today?"

"Yes, Your Honor." I responded.

"Do you understand that this holds the same legality as the order of protection and should he violate this, he will be arrested?"

"Yes, Your Honor."

"Mr. Wilson's attorney has asked for a special modification of this order. In the event Jean Louise Wilson becomes ill, and is in the hospital, or a funeral home. Mr. Wilson may encounter you without consequences. Do you consent to this, Mrs. Wilson?"

"Yes, I will never be visiting Jean Louise Wilson in a hospital, and definitely not a funeral home either." I replied.

Jon elbowed me, but I didn't care. Jean Louise Wilson caught her son sexually assaulting me on several occasions. He can visit her bedside in a hospital, say his goodbyes at a funeral, but I've already found peace with the situation. I want nothing to do with Jean Louise Wilson, ever again.

"I have also included that if Mr. Wilson needs to visit his mother, he will enter her driveway from Marywood Boulevard, and he will remain in her residence during the duration of his entire visit. He will not have contact you, Lizzy, or Jayden."

"Thank you." I responded.

She dismissed me from the courtroom, where Latrine would then enter and sign his agreement. He signed the agreement so that Amanda would not have to hear the details of the things he did to me. No innocent person would give up offering a defense to such "accusations". Latrine knew what he did to me, and he wanted me to go away.

CHAPTER 22 UNRESOLVED TRAUMA

"Enola, how could you do this?" My grandmother phoned me. I had awaited this phone call for a few months.

"Do what?"

"Keep Latrine away from me, because you're mad at Cassidy?"

Surely, she was not going this route with me again. I was now a thirty-two-year-old woman, that for sure knew right from wrong. Surely, she was not ready to go here with me again, all these years later.

"I haven't talked to Cassidy in over two years, set aside texting her the court date, which you know by now, she didn't show up to. Stop blaming this on my mother. She's twelve hundred miles away because I held her accountable, right there with you and Latrine." I didn't give her an opportunity to talk over me, she had done that my entire life. "She runs from her problems, just like you. She drinks, causes more problems, and then runs. You guys are cowards."

"You just think your pussy doesn't stink?" My grandmother was raunchy with her answers sometimes. Especially when she drinks.

"Don't talk to me that way, you're disgusting. I know it does not stink, because I sleep with my husband and not my uncle and cousins. That's why you guys don't like me. I am different from all of you. You keep covering this shit up, Grandma, but I'm going to keep talking about it, until it stops."

"Enola, get real, you are the one with the problem. Latrine was a kid when he hurt you. He thought he was playing. He knows better now."

"Grandma, he did not tell me not to tell me when played soccer in the yard." I responded.

"So, what's your point Enola, Jesus Christ." She became agitated.

"My point is Latrine threatened my life if I told. He knew it was wrong. He always knew it was wrong."

"Enola, maybe you should leave this behind you now. Not for me, not for Latrine, but for you. I know you have had a rough life." My grandmother was attempting to twist this.

"So, you are acknowledging your son raped me?" I asked.

"Whatever you call it, and my daughter treating you so bad." She responded.

"You treat me bad too. I have tried to mend our relationship. I let you love my babies, I let you love me. You never deserved any of us."

"Grandma doesn't treat anybody bad. I'm dying, Enola."

ENOLA

"If you're dying, you should really try to mend the things you have taken part in breaking with me. My innocent little soul. I'm begging from the inside to be worthy of an apology from you one day. It breaks me sometimes." I never wanted her to know she had the ability of making me feel that way, but I had broken down and told her anyways.

"You keep those babies from me us. Don't go there." She became defensive. Our conversations always escalated quickly.

"I kept them from everyone, but you, Grandma. You know it." I backed her into a corner. She could no longer lie to me about a situation I had created. She could no longer manipulate me.

"You think your kids are better than Skyla's?"

Here we go. Now is when I should hang the phone up, but instead I'll argue with her, one last time.

"No, but unlike Skyla, I will protect them. She takes Lylah to Latrine's. She is on the internet twerking in his living room, but I am the problem? No, the problem is you all gather at the family pedophiles house with all your children still... and then you accuse me of being stuck up for protecting mine. You guys are all sick."

"The family pedophile is JJ." Grandma insulted me once more.

"Yeah, you are right, the family pedophile is JJ, and then he taught Bozo to be it, and now, it's your son, Latrine. The silent rapist."

"A bit dramatic, Enola?"

"No, what was a bit dramatic was your son, forcing himself inside of me at five years old. That, was a bit dramatic."

"Disgusting. You are disgusting."

"No, Grandma, you are. You all need help. I never want to hear from you again after I hang this phone up." I meant it. I meant every word I had just spoken to her. Dying? I was not missing a chance to tell her exactly how I felt. I hung the phone up on my grandmother. She called back. This infuriated me.

"What?" I answered.

"I was in the hospital the week before your little unnecessary court date, you are going to kill me faster than this COPD." She quickly spoke.

"I am not going to kill you, the truth about what your son did to me, while you were supposed to be keeping me safe, might though."

"Stop this, Enola."

"Don't call back Grandma." I hung up again. I blocked her numbers from my phone so that she could not call back.

I took a deep breath. I vowed to never speak another word to my grandmother again. She had revictimized me time and time again, all my life.

"Hello?" I answered.

"Enola..." It was Jon.

"No bad news, right?" I asked. We had not been back from court long.

"No, but I'm reading through our file. I have a question, Enola."

"Ask."

"In this box, you wrote, very descriptively, the details of you uncle's tattoos..."

"Right, I didn't want to leave anything out."

"You later stated that he got these tattoos while he was in prison."

"Yeah, he did Jon."

"Ok, Enola, did he assault you after he returned home from prison?"

My mind raced. Nobody had ever asked me this.

"I don't think so, why?"

"Enola, you could only know those details so precisely, if you had seen them up close. Enola, the location of these tattoos, he would have had to have been nude for you to see them."

I didn't answer.

"Enola, I'm analyzing this for civil litigation." He explained further.

"Right." I responded.

"Enola, if he touched you for the last time at eleven, how do you know the details of the tattoos he got when you were fourteen?" Jon asked.

"Can I call you back?"

"Sure, trouble, we have some work to do, I think."

"Bye, Jon."

I hung the phone up. A thousand memories raced through my mind. I sat on the opposite end of the phone silently. What could I say? I knew what the tattoos looked like because Latrine, had indeed, assaulted me again as a teenager. A truth I had continued to deny. He was much bigger, as he had gained some muscle in prison. Amanda was downstairs asleep in the dungeon. She was literally right underneath of us. I nor Amanda were supposed to be around Latrine, as the judge had said no minor females, period. My mother and grandmother disregarded this and allowed me there anyways. The memories were pouring in. There I was, replaying the incident, I had long denied.

I was fast asleep, the the spare bedroom upstairs of my grandmother's home. Latrine came in, in the middle of the night. I was sexually active by this point, and I had snuck Melvin into my grandparents' house many times before. I felt a hand down my panties, and a finger enter my vagina.

"Melvin?" It was pitch black and I could not see.

"No, shhh--."

"Latrine, what are you doing?" I panicked. My mother had specifically told me to stay away from Latrine. I was to only sleep upstairs. He did not care.

"Enola, one more time." He attempted to remove my underwear. I fought him and pulled them back up. "I won't make you. You're a woman now." He spoke softly in my ear. Latrine inserted his fingers back inside of me.

"No." I clearly and concisely spoke.

"Yes."

"No means no, Latrine." I never let up.

"Do you really want me to stop?" He asked, still moving his fingers in and out of me.

"I want you to stop it, right now." I was petrified. I suddenly felt like that lost, helpless little girl again.

He got up and quietly exited the room. The damage was already redone though. Anything I had healed from, was just taken from me again. All I was doing, was sleeping over at my grandmothers again.

I vowed to never tell anyone these things, until now. Later that night I got up; the house was quiet and still. I walked down the stairs and opened the door to the dungeon where he and Amanda slept. I turned the light on, which did not wake either of them up. I studied every inch of Jesus' face newly tattooed on Latrine's chest. I had gone into the dungeon with the intentions of exposing Latrine to Amanda, but when they didn't wake up, rather I stood there. My mind raced to places it had never been. Intrusive thoughts took over. I possessed a skill of life that the rest of the family had not, to control my own actions. I realized now it was not safe for anybody, me spending the night there. I quietly snuck out of my grandmothers' home and walked to my father's. He was confused the next morning as to what had led me there. I never told anyone, until now. We are only as dark as the secrets we keep. Free your mind.

ABOUT THE AUTHOR

K.D.Weaver (Katey) is a mother, wife, coach, mentor, and advocate who began writing short stories as soon as she was able to hold a pencil correctly. Katey is the once victim of childhood sexual abuse. She is a victim of rape, incest, and child molestation. She grew popular on a trending social media site during the global pandemic. Her viewers were attracted to her rare style of sharing her story. Weaver had begun writing an autobiography in her late high school years. During her adult life she turned that unfinished autobiography into a finished book, based on a true story, of course. Weaver would like to educate people around the world about sexual abuse. During her journey of self-healing, she was faced with many unexpected truths. After reading counseling notes from her youth, she realized the best way for her to heal, was to understand her childhood, and what better way to do it, than to write it all down. She always had a huge passion for writing and a story to tell.

Printed in Great Britain
by Amazon

79467703R00068